THE COMEDIES OF
WILLIAM SHAKESPEARE

SHAKESPEARE
HIS WORK AND WORLD

THE COMEDIES OF WILLIAM SHAKESPEARE

EDITED BY KATHLEEN KUIPER, SENIOR EDITOR, ARTS AND CULTURE

Britannica® Educational Publishing
IN ASSOCIATION WITH
ROSEN EDUCATIONAL SERVICES

Published in 2013 by Britannica Educational Publishing
(a trademark of Encyclopædia Britannica, Inc.)
in association with Rosen Educational Services, LLC
29 East 21st Street, New York, NY 10010.

Distributed exclusively by Rosen Educational Services.
For a listing of additional Britannica Educational Publishing titles, call toll free (800) 237-9932.

First Edition

Britannica Educational Publishing
Adam Augustyn: Assistant Manager
J.E. Luebering: Senior Manager
Marilyn L. Barton: Senior Coordinator, Production Control
Steven Bosco: Director, Editorial Technologies
Lisa S. Braucher: Senior Producer and Data Editor
Yvette Charboneau: Senior Copy Editor
Kathy Nakamura: Manager, Media Acquisition
Kathleen Kuiper: Senior Editor, Arts and Culture

Rosen Educational Services
Jeanne Nagle: Senior Editor
Nelson Sá: Art Director
Cindy Reiman: Photography Manager
Amy Feinberg: Photo Researcher
Brian Garvey: Designer and Cover Design
Introduction by Adam Augustyn

Library of Congress Cataloging-in-Publication Data

The comedies of William Shakespeare/edited by Kathleen Kuiper.—1st ed.
p. cm.—(Shakespeare: his work and world)
"In association with Britannica Educational Publishing, Rosen Educational Services."
Includes bibliographical references and index.
ISBN 978-1-61530-928-3 (library binding)
1. Shakespeare, William, 1564-1616—Comedies. I. Kuiper, Kathleen.
PR2981.C58 2013
822.3'3—dc23

2012029319

Manufactured in the United States of America

On the cover: Cast members from a German production of *A Midsummer Night's Dream* perform at the 2007 Salzburg Festival. *AFP/Getty Images*

Pages 1, 20, 35, 55, 76, 95, 109 Hulton Archive/Getty Images

Contents

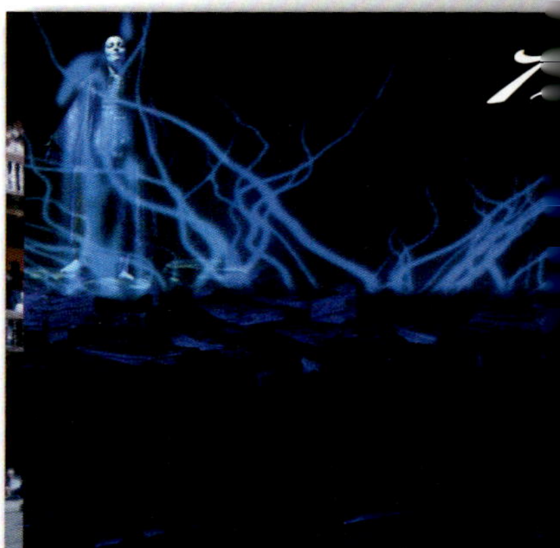

90

96

106

Introduction

Some people do not consider William Shakespeare's comedies to be his most important works. This is not because the comedies lack merit, but because of the sheer number of great tragedies he produced. Readers generally also concede that the word *great* does not apply to a genre that, by definition, provides lighter fare. Nevertheless, it must be asserted that Shakespeare's comedies indeed contain a wealth of genius; comedic characters such as Puck (*A Midsummer Night's Dream*), Beatrice (*Much Ado About Nothing*), and Viola (*Twelfth Night*) are among the Bard's most fully realized and lasting creations. A close examination of his comedies, as detailed in this book, lends credence to this assertion.

Comedy is a class of literature that is sometimes difficult to categorize, although that has not prevented a number of authorities from attempting to do just that, as well as to distinguish a clear line between comedy and tragedy. Most people assume that "comedy" is synonymous with "funny," but this is not necessarily so. While works in the genre usually are amusing, that is not comedy's defining feature. Instead, comedy was described by the ancient Greeks, notably Aristotle, as art that concerns humans as social beings interacting with others, as opposed to considering them as private individuals. Other unifying features of comedies are a focus on lowborn people, imitations of nature, and a grounded appraisal of the inherent contradictions of life.

Statue of a fool standing outside the Globe Theatre in London. Fools make an appearance in many of Shakespeare's plays, including his comedies Twelfth Night *and* As You Like It. Francie Manning/Photolibrary/Getty Images

Shakespeare's first plays were primarily histories and comedies. His early works in the latter genre are often classed as romantic comedies since their plots are primarily driven by the pursuit of love, as in *The Two Gentlemen of Verona*, which is considered by some scholars to be his very first completed play. The play's plot revolves around the titular men, Valentine and Proteus, who travel to Milan, where they are educated in courtly behaviour. Complicated relationships develop between the two gentlemen and the characters Sylvia (the Duke of Milan's daughter, who is in love with Valentine and eventually pursued by Proteus) and Julia (Proteus's love who secretly poses as his page in Milan). In the fourth act, a device that later became a prominent theme in Shakespearean comedies develops: the characters leave civilization and journey into nature, where the inhibitions of public life are stripped away. In the wild they both knowingly and unknowingly tap into primal behaviours, such as when Proteus attempts to rape Sylvia, the resistant object of his affections. The play ends after Valentine shames Proteus for his actions and thus reintroduces civilized deportment, which results in the four young lovers coupling off in their original pairs and living in "mutual happiness."

The Comedy of Errors takes the "confused identity" plotline of Julia in *The Two Gentlemen of Verona* and expands it throughout the play. The plot revolves around two sets of identical twins (sons of a merchant, Egeon, and their servants) that get paired off in a storm and raised apart from their respective brothers. The four end up in the same city by happenstance years later, just as Egeon is about to be put to death for his inability to pay a ransom. A series of misidentifications ensue, but the play ends with identities sorted out, the brothers happily reunited, and Egeon pardoned.

Shakespeare tweaked the standard romantic comedy formula with his next comedy, *Love's Labour's Lost*, which tells the story of four young men who decide to focus on the life of the mind to the exclusion of romantic entanglements. Of course, they soon meet four young women who are not only comely but can easily match wits with them. The drama shows the men falling for the women, but just as the "happily ever after" moment seems at hand, Shakespeare upsets the audience's expectations by introducing an off-stage death that forces the ladies back home. *Love's Labour's Lost* thus ends with the hope of a reunification of the couples in a year's time, but no guarantee that the event will in fact happen.

One of Shakespeare's most-adapted comedies is *The Taming of the Shrew*. The story of a difficult daughter who must be married off before her much-courted younger sister may marry has been the plot of countless literary works over the centuries. Shakespeare's play revolves around the sisters Katharina, a headstrong woman who is being courted by the clever Petruchio, and Bianca, who is being wooed by three men. While modern adaptations of the play are typically light-hearted and playful, the original has a harsh denouement that sees Petruchio "tame" Katharina after their marriage by depriving her of food, sleep, and other necessities in an effort to teach her "wifely obedience." Bianca's plot ends with her wed and taking on her sister's former shrewish nature. Although the principal characters are paired off, the ideal comedic happy ending is never quite reached, and the ending is far from merry.

The most popular of Shakespeare's "return to nature" comedies is *A Midsummer Night's Dream*, the tale of a group of city-dwellers from Athens and their interactions with the residents of an enchanted forest. The young urban couples have their desires guided by the mischievous magic of Puck, a forest fairy armed with a love potion. After a series of misplaced affections and comedic misunderstandings, order is restored by Oberon, the king of the fairies, and the play ends with a celebratory triple wedding for the Athenians. Once again, the removal of the trappings of contemporary society and the immersion into a "natural" rural space acts as a catalyst to compel the principals into conventional (and, pointedly, male-dominated) heterosexual coupling.

A much less conventional comedy is *The Merchant of Venice*. The play tells the story of Bassanio who requests a loan from his friend Antonio (the titular merchant) who, in turn, borrows money from Shylock, a Jewish moneylender. Shylock famously demands a pound of Antonio's flesh if he cannot repay the loan on time, which is indeed what comes to pass. Antonio escapes his certain death when Portia, Bassanio's beloved, saves the day. Posing as a lawyer, she points out that Shylock may have Antonio's flesh only, but if he spills any blood in the process he faces punishment under Venetian law. A compromise is then reached and Shylock is forced to convert to Christianity as part of his penance. However, Bassanio and Antonio's victory rings hollow as the play makes it clear that Shylock was first put into his vengeful mindset after years of mistreatment by Venice's Christians, and his punishment is simply additional humiliation. A second plot that follows Bassanio as he woos and eventually wins Portia gives the play its comedic character, but Shylock's tragic story and his poignant pleas for equal treatment of Jews ("If you prick us, do we not bleed?") overshadows the Portia-Bassanio story line and pushes the play into the category of tragicomedy.

Much Ado About Nothing returns to Shakespeare's familiar milieu of the battle of the sexes. The play centres on two couples: Hero and Claudio, a conventional love-struck pair, and Beatrice and Benedick, two jaded individuals with little interest in marriage who engage in a battle of wits over the course of the drama. The clever interaction between Beatrice and Benedick is the most compelling aspect of the play; the two former cynics eventually fall in love via their constant bantering. Meanwhile, Claudio's jealous friend Don John convinces him that Hero has been unfaithful, and Claudio publicly jilts her at their wedding ceremony. The plot takes a somber turn as Hero's humiliated family fakes her death and her cousin Beatrice attempts to convince her new lover Benedick to kill Claudio. However, Don John's treachery is uncovered in time to produce a typically light comedic ending. The play is especially notable for its depiction of equal intellectual footing in the Beatrice-Benedick relationship, which acts as a progressive counterbalance to Shakespeare's earlier treatment of women in his *Taming of the Shrew*.

Shakespeare's *As You Like It* takes places primarily in one of his familiar pastoral spaces, the Forest of Arden. The forest is home to a Duke and his followers, who were forced into exile when the Duke's brother usurped his court. The group is soon joined by Orlando, who fled the court to escape his own treacherous brother, and Rosalind, the Duke's daughter. For her safety while in the forest, Rosalind disguises herself as a young man named Ganymede. Thus disguised she befriends Orlando, her lover at court. "Ganymede" counsels Orlando and directs him toward a more realistic conception of love. Orlando's brother Oliver arrives at camp intending to kill Orlando but has a change of heart after his brother saves him from an attack by wild animals. A penitent Oliver then falls for Rosalind's disguised cousin, and a group wedding ends the work once the young women reveal their true identities.

The prevailing through-line of *As You Like It* is that true love is not formal and prescribed but delightfully foolish, more at home in the wilds of Arden than in the courts of lords and ladies.

The main plot of *Twelfth Night; or, What You Will* also centres on a female disguised as a male. In this play, a shipwrecked Viola, who was separated from her presumed-lost twin brother Sebastian in the accident, dresses as a young man and takes on the name Cesario in order to join the court of Duke Orsino. There, she falls for Orsino, who later sends "Cesario" to express his love to the lady Olivia. She instead becomes enamoured of "Cesario," and Orsino and "Cesario" enter into an unwitting competition for Olivia's hand, a circumstance further complicated by the burgeoning camaraderie between the two. Once again Shakespeare features the disguised female giving cloaked love advice to the target of her affections. A miraculously saved Sebastian arrives on the scene, and Olivia immediately proposes to him, initially thinking that he is his disguised sister. Viola's true identity is revealed and, once again, same-sex friendship is transformed into lasting heterosexual union.

The Merry Wives of Windsor is a departure from Shakespeare's comedies of this era in that it takes place not in a fictional location, but in Windsor, England. It is also unusual in that he brings back characters from his earlier history plays—notably the bawdy and popular Falstaff—and inserts them into the action. The play's plot revolves around Falstaff's romantic pursuit of two married women (Mistress Ford and Mistress Page) in the hopes of swindling money from them. The two wives learn of his scheme plan a series of ruses to trick Falstaff. The play resolves with a humiliated Falstaff being forgiven and Mistress Page's daughter paired off with a worthy suitor.

At the turn of the century, Shakespeare began exploring darker subject matter in his dramas. This period saw him produce his great tragedies, as well as a selection of dramas known as the "problem plays" that scholars have had difficulty classifying for centuries. Two of these works—*All's Well That Ends Well* and *Measure for Measure*—are traditionally grouped with the comedies. (The third problem play, *Troilus and Cressida*, is usually classed as a tragedy.) The "comedic" problem plays share many plot elements, including hidden identities, broken engagements, characters surreptitiously replacing others in their desired partner's bed, and nominally happy resolutions reached via morally ambiguous means.

After the problem plays, Shakespeare wrote the last of his comedies, producing four plays that are known as the romances for their common plots involving separation and reunions, as well as for an abundant use of mythic and fantastical elements. The first of the romances, *Pericles*, presages a common theme of Shakespeare's later tragedies: the relationship between parents and their children, particularly that of fathers and daughters. While sailing back to his homeland, Tyre, after his wedding, Pericles encounters a violent storm, during which his wife gives birth to a daughter, Marina. Believing that his wife has died in childbirth, he buries her at sea. Still alive, she is rescued and joins a temple of the goddess Diana. The grief-stricken Pericles leaves Marina to be raised by the governor of Tarsus, and he returns to Tyre to rule. The plot is picked up years later as Marina is kidnapped by pirates and sold to a brothel. There, she meets up with her sickly father, who then has a vision of Diana. He and Marina sail to his wife's temple and the play ends with a joyous family reunion.

The other romances—*The Winter's Tale*, *Cymbeline*, and *The Tempest*—follow a similar pattern of familial separation, disconsolation, and bittersweet reunion. The most notable of this trio is *The Tempest*, which not only features the most prevalent introduction of the supernatural in the play's protagonist, the magician Prospero, but also contains the strongest father-daughter connection of all the romances. The play also makes explicit the connection between Prospero, whose machinations drive the play's plot, and Shakespeare himself. *The Tempest* was intended to be his farewell to theatre, and it is therefore filled with reflective passages on the power of art and a prevailing sense of closure. Because Shakespeare's valedictory work hews closely to the Classical definition of drama, it seems clear that he intended to end his own career with the standard comedic denouement that he wrote for his on-stage surrogate: a happy ending.

Chapter 1

The Art of Comedy

The classic conception of comedy—which began with Aristotle in ancient Greece of the 4th century BCE, continued through Shakespeare's time, and persists to the present—holds that comedy is primarily concerned with humans as social beings, rather than as private persons, and that its function is frankly corrective. The comic artist's purpose is to hold a mirror up to society to reflect its follies and vices in the hope that they will, as a result, be mended. The 20th-century French philosopher Henri Bergson shared this view of the corrective purpose of laughter; specifically, he felt, laughter is intended to bring the comic character back into conformity with his society, whose logic and conventions he abandons when "he slackens in the attention that is due to life."

ORIGINS AND DEFINITIONS

The word *comedy* seems to be connected by derivation with the Greek verb meaning "to revel," and comedy arose out of the revels associated with the rites of Dionysus, the god of nature, wine, and ecstasy. Aristotle, in his *Poetics*, states that comedy originated in phallic songs and that, like tragedy, it began in improvisation. Though tragedy evolved by stages that can be traced, the progress of comedy passed unnoticed because—poetically enough—it was not taken seriously. When the concepts of tragedy and comedy

Gold mask representing comedy, usually paired with a mask representing tragedy as a universal symbol of the theatre. iStockphoto/ Thinkstock

arose, poets wrote one or the other, according to their natural bent. Those of the graver sort, who might previously have been inclined to celebrate the actions of the great in epic poetry, turned to tragedy. Poets who had set forth the doings of the ignoble commoner using invectives (insults) typically turned to comedy. The distinction is basic to the Aristotelian differentiation between tragedy and comedy: Tragedy imitates those who are better than the average and comedy those who are worse.

For centuries, efforts at defining comedy were to be along the lines set down by Aristotle: the view that tragedy deals with personages of high estate, and comedy deals with lowly types; that tragedy deals with matters of great public import, while comedy is concerned with the private affairs of mundane, ordinary life; and that the characters and events of tragedy are historic and so, in some sense, true, while the humbler materials of comedy are but feigned. Implicit, too, in Aristotle is the distinction in styles deemed appropriate to the treatment of tragic and comic story. As long as there was at least a theoretical separation of comic and tragic styles, either genre could, on occasion, appropriate the stylistic manner of the other to a striking effect; the effect lost its lustre after the crossing of stylistic lines became commonplace.

The ancient Roman poet Horace, who wrote on such stylistic differences, noted the special effects that can be achieved when comedy lifts its voice in pseudotragic rant or when tragedy adopts the prosaic but affecting language of comedy. Consciously combined, the mixture of styles produces the burlesque, in which the grand manner (epic or tragic) is applied to a trivial subject, or the serious subject is subjected to a vulgar treatment, to ludicrous effect.

The English novelist Henry Fielding, in the preface to *Joseph Andrews* (1742), was careful to distinguish between the comic and the burlesque. The latter centres on the monstrous and unnatural, and gives pleasure through the surprising absurdity exhibited in appropriating the manners of the highest to the lowest, or vice versa. Comedy, on the other hand, confines itself to the imitation of nature, and, according to Fielding, the comic artist is not to be excused for deviating from it. The comic artist's subject is the ridiculous, not the monstrous, and the nature that artist is to imitate is human nature, as viewed in the ordinary scenes of civilized society.

THE HUMAN CONTRADICTION

In dealing with humans as social beings, all great comic artists—with Shakespeare among the greatest—have known that they are in the presence of a contradiction: that behind the social being lurks an animal being, whose behaviour often accords very ill with the canons dictated by society. Comedy, from its ritual beginnings, has celebrated creative energy. The primitive revels out of which comedy arose frankly acknowledged the animal nature of human beings; the animal masquerades and the phallic processions are the obvious witnesses to it. Comedy testifies to physical vitality, delight in life, and the will to go on living. In Shakespeare's plays in particular, comedy is at its merriest, its most festive, when this rhythm of life can be affirmed within the civilized context of human society. In the absence of this sort of harmony between creatural instincts and the dictates of civilization, sundry strains and discontents arise, all bearing witness to the contradictory nature of humanity, which in the comic view is a radical dualism; efforts to follow the way of rational sobriety are forever being interrupted by the infirmities of the flesh. The duality that tragedy views as a fatal contradiction in the nature of things, comedy views as one more instance of the incongruous reality that everyone must live with as best they can.

"Wherever there is life, there is contradiction," says Søren Kierkegaard, the 19th-century Danish existentialist, in the *Concluding Unscientific Postscript* (1846), "and wherever there is contradiction, the comical is present." He went on to say that the tragic and the comic are both based on contradiction but "the tragic is the suffering contradiction, comical, painless contradiction." Comedy makes the contradiction manifest along with a way out, which is why the contradiction is painless. Tragedy, on the other hand, despairs of a way out of the contradiction.

COMEDY, SATIRE, AND ROMANCE

Comedy's dualistic view of the individual as an incongruous mixture of bodily instinct and rational intellect is an essentially ironic view—implying the capacity to see things in a double aspect. The comic drama takes on the features of satire as it fixes on professions of virtue and the practices that contradict them. Satire assumes standards against which professions and practices are judged. To the extent that the professions prove hollow and the practices vicious, the ironic perception darkens and deepens. The element of the incongruous points in the direction of the grotesque, which implies an admixture of elements that do not match. The ironic gaze eventually penetrates to a vision of the grotesque quality of experience, marked by the discontinuity of word and deed and the total lack of coherence between appearance and reality. This suggests one of the extreme limits of comedy, the satiric extreme, in which the sense of the discrepancy between things as they are and things as they might be or ought to be has reached to the borders of tragedy. For the tragic apprehension, as Kierkegaard states, despairs of a way out of the contradictions that life presents.

As satire may be said to govern the movement of comedy in one direction, romance governs its movement in the other. Satiric comedy dramatizes the discrepancy between the ideal and the reality and condemns the pretensions that would mask reality's hollowness and viciousness. Romantic comedy also regularly presents the conflict between the ideal shape of things as the hero or heroine could wish them to be and the hard realities with which they are confronted, but typically it ends by invoking the ideal, despite whatever difficulties reality has put in its way. This is never managed without a good deal of contrivance, and the plot of the typical romantic comedy is a medley of clever scheming, calculated coincidence, and wondrous discovery, all of which contribute ultimately to making the events answer precisely to the hero's or heroine's wishes.

TRAGICOMEDY

Since about 1580, dramatic works incorporating both tragic and comic elements generally have been referred to as tragicomedies. When coined by the Roman dramatist Plautus in the 2nd century BCE, the word denoted a play in which gods and mortals, masters, and slaves reverse the roles traditionally assigned to them, gods and heroes acting in comic burlesque and slaves adopting tragic dignity. This startling innovation may be seen in Plautus's *Amphitryon*.

In the Renaissance, tragicomedy became a genre of play that mixed tragic elements into drama that was mainly comic. The Italian writer Battista Guarini defined tragicomedy as having most of tragedy's elements—e.g., a certain gravity of diction, the depiction of important public events, and the arousal of compassion—but never carrying the action to tragedy's conclusion, and judiciously including such comic elements as low-born characters, laughter, and jests. Central to this kind of tragicomedy were danger, reversal, and a happy ending. Despite its affront to the strict Neoclassicism of the day, which forbade the mixing of genres, tragicomedy flourished, especially in England, whose writers largely ignored the edicts of Neoclassicism. John Fletcher provides a good example of the genre in *The Faithful Shepherdess* (*c.* 1608), itself a reworking of Guarini's *Il pastor fido*, first published in 1590. Notable examples of tragicomedy by William Shakespeare are *The Merchant of Venice*, *The Winter's Tale*, and *The Tempest*.

Nineteenth-century Romantic writers espoused Shakespeare's use of tragicomedy in the belief that his plays closely mirrored nature, and they used him as a model for their works. The dramas of Georg Büchner, Victor Hugo, and Christian Dietrich Grabbe reflect his influence. With the advent of realism later in the 19th century, tragicomedy underwent yet another revision. Still intermingling the two elements, comic interludes now highlighted the ironic counterpoints inherent in a play, making the tragedy seem even more devastating. Such works as Henrik Ibsen's *Ghosts* (1881) and *The Wild Duck* (1884) reflect this technique. George Bernard Shaw said of Ibsen's work that it established tragicomedy as a more meaningful and serious entertainment than tragedy. Anton Chekhov's tragicomedies include *Uncle Vanya* (1897) and *The Cherry Orchard* (1904).

In the 20th century, tragicomedy was sometimes used synonymously with tragicomedyAbsurdist drama, which suggested that laughter is the only response left to humans when they are faced with the tragic emptiness and meaninglessness of existence. Important midcentury examples of this modern type of tragicomedy are Samuel Beckett's *Endgame* (1958) and Harold Pinter's *The Dumb-Waiter* (1960).

Shakespeare perhaps most fully explored the wide range of dramatic possibilities of the romantic mode of comedy. But plotting of the sort that appears in his plays has had a long stage tradition and not exclusively in comedy. It is first encountered in the tragicomedies of the ancient Greek dramatist Euripides (e.g., *Alcestis, Iphigenia Among the Taurians, Ion, Helen*). The means by which the happy ending is accomplished in romantic comedy—the document or the bodily mark that establishes identities to the satisfaction of all the characters of goodwill—are part of the stock-in-trade of all comic dramatists, even such 20th-century playwrights as Jean Anouilh (in *Traveler Without Luggage*, 1937) and T.S. Eliot (in *The Confidential Clerk*, 1953).

There is nothing necessarily inconsistent in the use of a calculatedly artificial dramatic design to convey a serious dramatic statement. The contrived artifice of Shakespeare's mature comic plots is the perfect foil against which the reality of the characters' feelings and attitudes assumes the greater naturalness. The strange coincidences, remarkable discoveries, and wonderful reunions are unimportant compared with the emotions of relief and awe that they inspire. Their function, as Shakespeare uses them, is precisely to give rise to such emotions, and the emotions, thanks to the plangent poetry in which they are expressed, end by transcending the circumstances that occasioned them. But when such artifices are employed simply for the purpose of eliminating the obstacles to a happy ending—as is the case in the sentimental comedy of the 18th and early 19th centuries—then they stand forth as imaginatively impoverished dramatic clichés.

THEORIES OF COMEDY

The treatise that Aristotle is presumed to have written on comedy is lost. There is, however, a fragmentary treatise on comedy that bears an obvious relation to Aristotle's treatise on tragedy, *Poetics*, and is generally taken to be either a version of a lost Aristotelian original or an expression of the philosophical tradition to which he belonged. This is the *Tractatus Coislinianus*, preserved in a 10th-century manuscript in the Coislin collection of Greek manuscripts in Paris. The *Tractatus* divides the substance of comedy into the same six elements that are discussed in regard to tragedy in the *Poetics*: plot, character, thought, diction, melody, and spectacle. The characters of comedy, according to the *Tractatus*, are of three kinds: the impostors, the self-deprecators, and the buffoons. The Aristotelian tradition from which the *Tractatus* derives probably provided a fourth, the churl, or boor. The list of comic characters in the *Tractatus* is closely related to a passage in Aristotle's *Nicomachean Ethics*, in which the boaster (the person who says more than the truth) is compared with the mock-modest (the person who says less), and the buffoon (who has too much wit) is contrasted with the boor (who has too little).

DIVINE COMEDIES IN THE WEST AND EAST

The 4th-century Latin grammarian Donatus distinguished comedy from tragedy by the simplest terms: comedies begin in trouble and end in peace, while tragedies begin in calms and end in tempest. Such a differentiation of the two genres may be simplistic, but it provided sufficient grounds for Dante to call his great poem *La Commedia* (*The Comedy*; later called *The Divine Comedy*), since, as he says in his dedicatory letter, it begins amid the horrors of hell but ends amid the pleasures of heaven. This suggests the movement of Shakespeare's last plays, which begin amid the distresses of the world and end in a supernal peace. Comedy conceived in this sublime and serene mode is rare but recurrent in the history of the theatre. The Spanish dramatist Pedro Calderón de la Barca's *Life Is a Dream* (1635) is an example. In later drama, Henrik Ibsen's *Little Eyolf* (1894) and August Strindberg's *To Damascus* (1898–1904)—both of which are late works of these Scandinavian dramatists—have affinities with this type. It may represent the most universal mode of comedy. The American philosopher Susanne K. Langer writes:

> In Asia the designation "Divine Comedy" would fit numberless plays; especially in India triumphant gods, divine lovers united after various trials [as in the perennially popular romance of Rama and Sita], are the favourite themes of a theater that knows no "tragic rhythm." The classical Sanskrit drama was heroic comedy—high poetry, noble action, themes almost always taken from the myths—a serious, religiously conceived drama, yet in the "comic" pattern, which is not a complete

(continued on page 10)

(continued from page 9)

organic development reaching a foregone, inevitable conclusion, but is episodic, restoring a lost balance, and implying a new future. The reason for this consistently "comic" image of life in India is obvious enough: both Hindu and Buddhist regard life as an episode in the much longer career of the soul which has to accomplish many incarnations before it reaches its goal, nirvana. Its struggles in the world do not exhaust it; in fact they are scarcely worth recording except in entertainment theater, "comedy" in our sense—satire, farce, and dialogue. The characters whose fortunes are seriously interesting are the eternal gods; and for them there is no death, no limit of potentialities, hence no fate to be fulfilled. There is only the balanced rhythm of sentience and emotion, upholding itself amid the changes of material nature. (From *Feeling and Form*; Charles Scribner's Sons, 1953.)

COMEDY AS RITE

The *Tractatus* was not printed until 1839, and its influence on comic theory is thus of relatively modern date. It is frequently cited in the studies that attempt to combine literary criticism and anthropology, in the manner in which James George Frazer combined studies of "primitive" religion and culture in *The Golden Bough* (1890–1915). In such works, comedy and tragedy alike are traced to a prehistoric death-and-resurrection ceremonial, a seasonal pantomime in which the old year, in the guise of an aged king (or hero or god), is killed, and the new spirit of fertility, the resurrection or initiation of the young king, is brought in. This rite typically featured a ritual combat, or agon, between the representatives of the old and the new seasons, a feast in which the sacrificial body of the slain king was devoured, a marriage between the victorious new king and his chosen bride, and a final triumphal procession in celebration of the reincarnation or resurrection of the slain god. Implicit in the whole ceremony is the ancient rite of purging the tribe through the expulsion of a scapegoat, who carries away the accumulated sins of the past year. Frazer, speaking of scapegoats in *The Golden Bough*, noted that this expulsion of devils was commonly preceded or followed by a period of general license, an abandonment of the ordinary restraints of society during which all offenses except the gravest go unpunished. This quality of Saturnalia is characteristic of comedy from ancient Greece through medieval Europe.

The seasonal rites that celebrate the yearly cycle of birth, death, and rebirth were seen by the Canadian critic Northrop Frye as the basis for the generic plots of comedy, romance, tragedy, and irony and satire. The four prefigure the fate of a hero and the society he brings into being. In comedy (representing the season of spring), the hero appears in a society controlled by obstructing characters and succeeds in wresting it from their grasp. The movement of comedy of this sort typically replaces falsehood with truth, illusion with reality. The hero, having come into possession of his new society, sets forth upon adventures, and these are the province of romance (summer). Tragedy (autumn) commemorates the hero's passion and death. Irony and satire (winter) depict a world from which the hero has disappeared, a vision of "unidealized existence." With spring, the hero is born anew.

THE MORAL FORCE OF COMEDY

The characters of comedy specified in the *Tractatus* arrange themselves in a familiar pattern: a clever hero is surrounded by fools of sundry varieties (impostors, buffoons, boors). The hero is something of a trickster; he dissimulates his own powers, while exploiting the weaknesses of those around him. The comic pattern is a persistent one; it appears not only in ancient Greek comedy but also in the farces of ancient Italy, in the commedia dell'arte that came into being in 16th-century Italy, and even in the routines of late-night television comedians and their sidekicks. Implicit here is the tendency to make folly ridiculous, to laugh it out of countenance, which has always been a prominent feature of comedy.

Renaissance critics, elaborating on the brief and cryptic account of comedy in Aristotle's *Poetics*, stressed the derisive force of comedy as an adjunct to morality. The Italian scholar Gian Giorgio Trissino's account of comedy in his *Poetica*, apparently written in the 1530s, is typical: as tragedy teaches by means of pity and fear, comedy teaches by deriding things that are vile. Attention is directed here, as in other critical treatises of this kind, to the source of laughter. According to Trissino, laughter is aroused by objects that are in some way ugly and especially by that from which better qualities were hoped. His statement suggests the relation of the comic to the incongruous. Trissino was as aware as the French poet Charles Baudelaire was three centuries later that laughter betokens the fallen nature of humans (Baudelaire would term it the Satanic nature). Human beings laugh, says Trissino (echoing Plato's dialogue *Philebus*), because they are envious and malicious and never delight in the good of others—except when those who laugh hope for some good from it for themselves.

The most important English Renaissance statement concerning comedy is that of Sir Philip Sidney in *The Defence of Poesie*, probably written in 1582—several years

Engraving by William Hogarth titled The Laughing Audience. *Playwrights and critics alike have raised several theories as to the nature of comedy, and what makes people laugh.* Time & Life Pictures/Getty Images

before Shakespeare composed his first plays—and published posthumously in 1595:

> Comedy is an imitation of the common errors of our life, which [the comic dramatist] representeth in the most ridiculous and scornful sort that may be, so as it is impossible that any beholder can be content to be such a one.

Like Trissino, Sidney notes that, while laughter comes from delight, not all objects of delight cause laughter, and he demonstrates the distinction as Trissino had done: "We are ravished with delight to see a fair woman, and yet are far from being moved to laughter. We laugh at deformed creatures, wherein certainly we cannot delight." The element of the incongruous is prominent in Sidney's account of scornful laughter. He cites the image of the hero of Greek legend Heracles, with his great beard and furious countenance, in woman's attire, spinning at the command of his beloved queen, Omphale, and declares that this arouses both delight and laughter.

COMEDY AND CHARACTER

Another English poet, John Dryden, in *Of Dramatick Poesie, an Essay* (1668), makes the same point in describing the kind of laughter produced by the ancient Greek comedy *The Clouds*, by Aristophanes. In it the character of Socrates is made ridiculous by acting very unlike the true Socrates—that is, by appearing childish and absurd rather than with the gravity of the true Socrates. Dryden was concerned with analyzing the laughable quality of comedy and with demonstrating the different forms it has taken in different periods of dramatic history. Aristophanic comedy sought its laughable quality not so much in the imitation of a person as in the representation of "some odd conceit that had commonly somewhat of unnatural or obscene in it." In the so-called New Comedy, introduced by Menander late in the 4th century BCE, writers sought to express the ethos, or character, as in their tragedies they expressed the pathos, or suffering, of humankind. This distinction goes back to Aristotle, who in the *Rhetoric* distinguished between ethos (natural bent, disposition, or moral character) and pathos (emotion) displayed in a given situation. And the Latin rhetorician Quintilian, in the 1st century CE, noted that ethos is akin to comedy and pathos to tragedy. The distinction is important to Renaissance and Neoclassical assumptions concerning the respective subject of comic and tragic representation. In terms of emotion, ethos is viewed as a permanent condition characteristic of the average person and relatively mild in its nature; pathos, on the other hand, is a temporary emotional state, often violent. Comedy thus expresses human character in the ordinary circumstances of everyday life, and tragedy expresses the sufferings of a particular individual in extraordinary periods of intense emotion.

In dealing with persons engaged in normal affairs, the comic dramatists tended to depict the individual in terms of some single but overriding personal trait or habit. They adopted a method based on the physiological concept of the four humours, or bodily fluids (blood, phlegm, choler, melancholy), and the belief that an equal proportion of these constituted health, while an excess or deficiency of any one of them brought disease. Since the humours governed temperament, an irregular distribution of them was considered to result not only in bodily sickness but also in derangements of personality and behaviour, as well. The resultant comedy of humours is distinctly English, as Dryden notes, and particularly identified with the comedies of Ben Jonson, perhaps the greatest of Shakespeare's contemporaries.

THE ROLE OF WIT

Humour is native to humankind. Folly need only be observed and imitated by the comic dramatist to give rise to laughter. Observers as early as the Roman rhetorician Quintilian (flourished 1st century CE), however, have pointed out that, though folly is laughable in itself, such jests may be improved if the writer adds something personal—namely, wit. A form of repartee, wit implies both a mental agility and a linguistic grace that is very much a product of conscious art. Quintilian describes wit at some length in his *Institutio oratoria*; it partakes of urbanity, a certain tincture of learning, charm, saltiness, or sharpness, and polish and elegance. In the preface (1671) to *An Evening's Love*, Dryden distinguishes between the comic talents of Jonson, on the one hand, and of Shakespeare and his contemporary John Fletcher, on the other, by virtue of their excelling respectively in humour and in wit. Jonson's talent lay in his ability "to make men appear pleasantly ridiculous on the stage," while Shakespeare and Fletcher excelled in wit, or "the sharpness of conceit," as seen in their repartee. The distinction is noted as well in *Of Dramatick Poesie, an Essay*, where a comparison is made between the character of Morose in Jonson's play *Epicoene*, who is characterized by his humour (namely, his inability to abide any noise but the sound of his own voice), and Shakespeare's Falstaff, who, according to Dryden, represents a miscellany of humours and is singular in saying things that are unexpected by the audience.

The distinctions that the English essayist William Hazlitt arrives at, then, in his "On Wit and Humour" (1819) are very much in the classic tradition of comic criticism:

> Humour is the describing the ludicrous as it is in itself; wit is the exposing it, by comparing or contrasting it with something else. Humour is, as it were, the growth of nature and accident; wit is the product of art and fancy.

The distinctions persist into the most sophisticated treatments of the subject. Sigmund Freud, for example, in *Wit and its Relation to the Unconscious* (1905), said that wit is made, but humour is found. Laughter, according to Freud, is aroused at actions that appear immoderate and inappropriate, at excessive expenditures of energy: it expresses a pleasurable sense of the superiority felt on such occasions.

FAILURE OF SELF-KNOWLEDGE

Aristotle said that comedy deals with the ridiculous, and Plato, in the *Philebus*, defined the ridiculous as a failure of self-knowledge; such a failure is there shown to be laughable in private individuals (the personages of comedy) but terrible in persons who wield power (the personages of tragedy). In comedy, the failure is often mirrored in a character's efforts to live up to an ideal of self that may be perfectly worthy but the wrong ideal for that particular character.

Shakespearean comedy is rich in examples: the King of Navarre and his courtiers, who must be made to realize that nature meant them to be lovers, not academicians, in *Love's Labour's Lost*; Beatrice and Benedick, who must be made to know that nature meant them for each other, not for the single life, in *Much Ado About Nothing*; Duke Orsino in *Twelfth Night*, who is brought to see that it is not Lady Olivia whom he loves but the disguised Viola, and Lady Olivia herself, who, when the right man comes along, decides that she will not dedicate herself to seven years of mourning for a dead brother, after all; and Angelo in *Measure for Measure*, whose image of himself collapses when his lust for Isabella makes it clear that he is not the ascetic type. The movement of all these plays follows a familiar comic pattern, wherein characters are brought from a condition of affected folly amounting to self-delusion to a plain recognition of who they are and what they want. For the five years or so after he wrote *Measure for Measure*, in 1603–04, Shakespeare seems to have addressed himself exclusively to tragedy, and each play in the sequence of masterpieces he produced during this period—*Othello*, *King Lear*, *Macbeth*, *Antony and Cleopatra*, and *Coriolanus*—turns in some measure on a failure of self-knowledge. This is notably so in the case of *Lear*, which is the tragedy of a man who (in the words of one of his daughters) "hath ever but slenderly known himself" and whose fault (as the Fool suggests) is to have grown old before he grew wise.

The plots of Shakespeare's last plays (*Pericles*, *Cymbeline*, *The Winter's Tale*, *The Tempest*) all contain a potential tragedy but one that is resolved by nontragic means. They contain, as well, an element of romance of the kind purveyed from Greek New Comedy through the plays of the ancient Roman comic dramatists Plautus and Terence. Children lost at birth are miraculously restored, years later, to their parents, thereby providing occasion for a recognition scene that functions as the denouement, or final outcome, of the plot. Characters find themselves—they come to know themselves—in all manner of ways by the ends of these plays. Tragic errors have been made, tragic losses have been suffered, tragic passions—envy, jealousy, wrath—have seemed to rage unchecked, but the miracle that these plays celebrate lies in the discovery that the errors can be forgiven, the losses restored, and the passions mastered by the godly spirit of reason. The near tragedies experienced by the characters result in the ultimate health and enlightenment of the soul. What is learned is of a profound simplicity: the need for patience under adversity, the need to repent of one's sins, the need to forgive the sins of others. In comedy of this high and sublime sort, patience, repentance, and forgiveness are opposed to the viciously circular pattern of crime, which begets vengeance, which begets more crime. Comedy of this sort deals in regeneration and rebirth. There is always about it something of the religious, as humankind is absolved of its guilt and reconciled one to another and to whatever powers that be.

Chapter 2

Shakespeare's Early Comedies

Other than *Titus Andronicus*, Shakespeare did not experiment with formal tragedy in his early years. (Though his English history plays from this period portrayed tragic events, their theme was focused elsewhere.) The young playwright was drawn more quickly into comedy, and with more immediate success. For this his models include the dramatists Robert Greene and John Lyly, along with Thomas Nashe. The result is a genre recognizably and distinctively Shakespearean, even if he learned a lot from Greene and Lyly: the romantic comedy. As in the work of his models, Shakespeare's early comedies revel in stories of amorous courtship in which a plucky and admirable young woman (played by a boy actor) is paired off against her male wooer.

THE TWO GENTLEMEN OF VERONA

This play was written perhaps in 1590–94 and published in the First Folio of 1623 from an authorial manuscript. It is a pastoral story about two young friends who travel to Milan, where they are educated in courtly behaviour.

The main source of the play's plot was a translation of a long Spanish prose romance titled *Los siete libros de la Diana* (1559?; *The Seven Books of the Diana*) by Jorge de Montemayor. Shakespeare is thought to have adapted the relationship of the two gentlemen of the title and the

SIR THOMAS ELYOT

(b. *c.* 1490—d. March 26, 1546, Carleton, Cambridgeshire, Eng.)

The English author and administrator Thomas Elyot was clerk to the Privy Council (1523–30) and was knighted in 1530. A member of humanist and statesman Sir Thomas More's circle, Elyot was suspected of being out of sympathy with Henry VIII's plan to divorce Catherine of Aragon and probably owed his lack of advancement to his friendship with More. In 1531 he published *The Boke Named the Governour*, dedicated to the king, and that autumn went as the king's envoy to the court of the Holy Roman emperor Charles V.

Elyot's popular *Governour*, a plan for the upbringing of gentlemen's sons who were to bear authority in the realm, was the first important English-language treatise on education and did much to form the later English ideal of the gentleman. His *Castel of Helth* was a popular regimen of health that, written in the vernacular and by a layman (although he had received some instruction in medicine), incurred censure but was widely read. His *Dictionary*, the first English dictionary of Classical Latin, was published in 1538. The aim of all Elyot's works was usefulness: he brought classics and Italian authors to the general public through his translations, he provided practical instruction in his own writings, and he added many new words to the English language. He was noted for his championship and use of English prose for subjects then customarily treated in Latin. Both as a philosopher and as a lexicographer, he endeavoured to "augment our Englysshe tongue" as a medium for ideas.

ending of the play from various possible sources, including Richard Edwards's play *Damon and Pythias* (1565), Geoffrey Chaucer's *The Knight's Tale* in *The Canterbury Tales*, and especially the story of Titus and Gisippus in Sir Thomas Elyot's *The Boke Named the Governour* (1531).

Valentine (one of the two gentlemen of the title) opens the play by chiding his closest friend, Proteus (the other gentleman), for remaining idly at home with his beloved Julia rather than venturing to Milan with him. Shortly thereafter Proteus's plans change, because of his father's insistence, and he, too, heads for Milan after proclaiming his undying love and fidelity to Julia.

Members of a cross-cultural theatre troupe performing a scene from Two Gentlemen of Verona *at the 2012 Globe to Globe international Shakespeare festival in London.* © AP Images

Mayhem erupts in the third act after the fickle Proteus arrives in Milan and abruptly becomes enamoured with Silvia, the Duke's fair daughter, with whom Valentine plans secretly to elope. Proteus treacherously betrays Valentine's plan to the Duke, who promptly banishes Valentine. The Duke is assisted in all this by Thurio, a wealthy and most unwelcome suitor to Silvia. Concurrently, Julia disguises herself as a boy and travels to Milan to be reunited with Proteus, only to discover him wooing Silvia for himself.

As the love entanglements ensue, the setting shifts from the civilized city to the forest. Silvia sets out to find Valentine, who has been captured by bandits and has agreed to become their leader. Silvia is accosted by the outlaws but is rescued by Proteus, who has been relentlessly following her with his page, the still-disguised Julia. Proteus then attempts to rape Silvia but is prevented by Valentine. The latter shames Proteus into penitence for his ruthless actions and inconstancy. In an extreme show of generosity and forgiveness, Valentine offers to give up Silvia for Proteus, causing Julia to faint and her identity to be revealed. Thus do the twin characteristics of generous friendship and enduring chaste loyalty of the two women bring Proteus to his senses. In the end, the men resolve to marry their original loves and live in "mutual happiness."

THE COMEDY OF ERRORS

This play was written in 1589–94 and first published in the First Folio of 1623 from Shakespeare's manuscript. It was based on *Menaechmi* ("Twins") by Plautus, with additional material from Plautus's *Amphitruo* and the story of Apollonius of Tyre. The play's comic confusions derive from the presence of twin brothers, unknown to each other, in the same town. Its twists of plot provide

PLAUTUS'S LEGACY

The Roman predecessors of Plautus in both tragedy and comedy borrowed most of their plots and all of their dramatic techniques from Greece. Plautus, like them, took most of his plots from plays written by Greek "New Comedy" authors of the late 4th and early 3rd centuries BCE, notably Menander and Philemon. Unlike his predecessors, however, Plautus did not borrow slavishly. Although the life represented in his plays is superficially Greek, the flavour is Roman, and Plautus incorporated into his adaptations Roman concepts, terms, and usages.

Even more important was his approach to the Latin language. His action was lively and slapstick, and he was able to marry the action to the word. In his hands, Latin became racy and colloquial, verse varied and choral. This approach helps Plautus's plays read like originals rather than adaptations.

In general, his plots simply provide a frame for scenes of pure farce, relying heavily on intrigue, mistaken identity, and similar devices. Plautus's comic effect springs from exaggeration, burlesque and often coarse humour, rapid action, and a deliberately upside-down portrayal of life, in which slaves give orders to their masters and parents are hoodwinked by their offspring. Despite these observations, it should be noted that no original texts by Plautus survive, though some 21 survive in "acting" versions. These had been adapted, modified, cut, expanded, and generally brought up-to-date for production purposes. Contemporary scholars admit the extreme improbability of ever establishing a "Plautine" text.

During the Middle Ages, Plautus was little read—if at all—in contrast to the popular Terence. By the mid-14th century, however, the humanist scholar and poet Petrarch knew eight of the comedies. As the remainder came to light, Plautus began to influence European domestic comedy, particularly after the Renaissance poet Ariosto had made the first imitations of Plautine comedy in the Italian vernacular. His influence was perhaps to be seen at its most sophisticated in the comedies of Molière (whose play *L'Avare*, for instance, was based on *Aulularia*), and it can be traced up to the 20th century in such adaptations as Jean Giraudoux's *Amphitryon 38* (1929), Cole Porter's musical *Out of This World* (1950), and the musical and motion picture *A Funny Thing Happened on the Way to the Forum* (1963). Plautus's stock character types have similarly had a long line of successors: the braggart soldier of *Miles Gloriosus*, for example, became the Capitano of the Italian commedia dell'arte, is recognizable in Nicholas Udall's *Ralph Roister Doister* (*c.* 1533), in Shakespeare's Pistol, and even in his Falstaff, as well as in other 19th- and 20th-century characters. Thus, Plautus, in adapting Greek New Comedy to Roman conditions and taste, also significantly affected the course of the European theatre.

suspense, surprise, expectation, and exhilaration and reveal Shakespeare's mastery of construction.

Egeon, a merchant of Syracuse, is arrested in Ephesus because of hostilities between the two cities and, unable to pay the local ransom, is condemned to death. He tells the duke, Solinus, his sad tale: years earlier he and his wife had been shipwrecked with their infant sons, identical twins, and a pair of infant servants, also identical twins. The parents, each with a son and a servant, were rescued but then permanently separated. Antipholus of Syracuse, the son raised by Egeon, has for five years been seeking his mother and brother, while Egeon in turn has been seeking his missing son. Egeon's story wins from Solinus a day's respite to raise the ransom money.

Shirley Jones looks on as Kelsey Grammer (left) *flogs Tom Hanks in a staged reading of* The Comedy of Errors *at a 2009 fund-raiser for the Shakespeare Festival/LA.* Ryan Miller/Getty Images

Meanwhile, Antipholus of Syracuse (with his servant, Dromio) has arrived in Ephesus, not knowing that his brother Antipholus of Ephesus (with his own servant, also named Dromio) is already there. A series of misidentifications ensue. Antipholus of Syracuse is entertained by his brother's wife and woos her sister; he receives a gold chain meant for his brother and is chased by a goldsmith for nonpayment. He and his servant hide in a priory, where they observe Egeon on his way to execution and recognize the priory's abbess as their mother, Emilia. The play ends happily with Egeon's ransom paid, true identities revealed, and the family reunited.

LOVE'S LABOUR'S LOST

Shakespeare wrote this play sometime between 1588 and 1597, more likely in the early 1590s. It was published in a quarto edition in 1598, with a title page suggesting that an earlier quarto had been lost. The 1598 quarto was printed seemingly from an authorial working draft showing signs of revision. The play's central comic device is that four young men, dedicated to study and the renunciation of women, meet four young women and inevitably abandon their unrealistic ideals.

The play opens as Ferdinand, the king of Navarre, and three of his noblemen—Berowne (Biron), Longaville, and Dumaine (Dumain)—debate their intellectual intentions. Their plans are thrown into disarray, however, when the Princess of France, attended by three ladies (Rosaline, Maria, and Katharine), arrives on a diplomatic mission from the king of France and must therefore be admitted into Navarre's park. The gentlemen soon discover that they are irresistibly attracted to the ladies. Their attempts at concealing their infatuations from one another are quickly exploded. Their next and more considerable problem, however, is to cope with the young ladies' devastating wit, through means of which the gentlemen are thoroughly put down.

Adding to this romantic landscape, Shakespeare provides a group of entertaining eccentrics: Nathaniel (the curate), Holofernes (a schoolmaster), Dull (the constable), Costard (the clown), Mote (or Moth, a page), and

COMMEDIA DELL'ARTE

The Italian theatrical form known as commedia dell'arte (Italian: "comedy of art") flourished throughout Europe from the 16th through the 18th century. Though it was more successful in France, where it became the Comédie-Italienne, it also made its mark in England, where elements from it were naturalized in the harlequinade in pantomime and in the Punch-and-Judy show, a puppet play involving the commedia dell'arte character Punch.

The commedia dell'arte was a form of popular theatre that emphasized ensemble acting. Its improvisations were set in a firm framework of masks and stock situations. Professional players who specialized in one role developed an unmatched comic acting technique, which contributed to the popularity of the itinerant commedia troupes that traveled throughout Europe. Despite contemporary depictions of scenarios and masks and descriptions of particular presentations, impressions today of what the commedia dell'arte was like are secondhand. The art is a lost one, its mood and style irrecoverable.

The first date certainly associated with an Italian commedia dell'arte troupe is 1545. The most famous early company was the Gelosi (1568–1604), and many other companies, such as the Desiosi, the Comici Confidènti, and the Uniti, followed. Each commedia dell'arte company had a stock of scenarios, commonplace books of soliloquies and witty exchanges, and about a dozen actors. Though there was some doubling of masks (roles), most players created their own masks or developed ones already established. This helped to keep a traditional continuity while allowing diversity.

Certain characters began as stock masks and developed into well-known characters in the hands of the most talented players. Among these were the Capitano, who developed into

Scaramouche; Pedrolino (or Pierrot); Arlecchino (Harlequin); and Pulcinella (related to the English Punchinello, or Punch). The zanni (stock servant characters, either comic rustics or witty fools) used certain tricks of their trade: practical jokes (burle)—often the fool, thinking he had tricked the clown, had the tables turned on him by a rustic wit as clever, if not so nimble, as his own—and comic business (lazzi).

An important legacy of the commedia dell'arte is its influence on other dramatic forms. Visiting commedia dell'arte troupes provided inspiration for other national dramatic forms to absorb the comic routines and plot devices of the commedia. Both Shakespeare and Ben Jonson incorporated stock characters and devices from the commedia dell'arte in their plays.

Jaquenetta (a country girl). Linking both groups is Don Adriano de Armado, a Spanish nobleman whose absurd pretensions to poetic eloquence and love melancholy are spent foolishly on the simple country girl, Jaquenetta. The play ends with a brilliant coup de théâtre (sudden turn of events) in the arrival of Marcade. His news of the death of the French king introduces into the never-never land of Navarre a note of sombre reality that reminds both the young ladies and the gentlemen that wooing and marriage entail serious responsibilities. Shakespeare's deliberate avoidance of the customary "and they all lived happily ever after" conclusion of the genre is remarkable: "Jack hath not Jill." To be sure, the audience is given a promise that the marriages will ultimately take place, after the gentlemen have had a year to think about themselves and come to maturity. Thus, the play ends with hope—perhaps the best kind of happy ending.

THE TAMING OF THE SHREW

This play was written sometime in 1590–94 and first printed in the First Folio of 1623. The play describes the volatile courtship between the shrewish Katharina (Kate) and the canny Petruchio, who is determined to subdue Katharina's legendary temper and win her dowry. The main story is offered as a play within a play. The frame plot consists of an initial two-scene "induction" in which a whimsical lord decides to play a practical joke on a drunken tinker, Christopher Sly, by inducing him to believe that he is in fact a nobleman who has suffered from amnesia and is only now awaking from it. The main body of the play is presented to Sly as an entertainment for his delectation.

The source of the Petruchio-Katharina plot is unknown, although a number of analogues exist in ballads about the "taming" of shrewish women. The play's other plot involving Bianca and her many suitors was derived from George Gascoigne's comedy *Supposes* (1566), itself a translation of *I suppositi* (1509) by Ludovico Ariosto.

Following the induction, the play opens in Padua, where several eligible bachelors have gathered to claim the hand of Bianca, the youngest daughter of the wealthy Baptista. But Baptista has stated that Bianca will not be wed before her older sister, Katharina. The plot of "the taming of the shrew" then begins when Petruchio arrives in Padua in search of a rich wife. His friend Hortensio sets Petruchio's sights on Katharina (the shrew). Although Katharina responds hostilely to Petruchio, he woos, wins, and tames her by the sheer force of his manly insistence and by his wit; Katharina is attracted to Petruchio in spite of herself, since clearly he is her match in a way that other men could not be. After their bizarre marriage ceremony, in which Petruchio dresses in a wild fashion and abuses the priest, Katharina's taming continues. In order to show

LUDOVICO ARIOSTO AND LATIN COMEDY

Ludovico Ariosto (1474–1533) showed an early inclination toward poetry, but his father intended him for a legal career, so he studied law, unwillingly, at Ferrara from 1489 to 1494. When his father died in 1500, Ludovico, as the eldest son, had to give up his dream of a peaceful life devoted to humanistic studies in order to provide for his siblings. In 1502 he became commander of the citadel of Canossa and in 1503 entered the service of Cardinal Ippolito d'Este, son of Duke Ercole I.

Ludovico Ariosto wearing a laurel crown, engraving. © Photos.com/Thinkstock

Ariosto's duties as a courtier in the duke's service were sharply at odds with his own simple tastes. He was expected to be in constant attendance on the cardinal and to accompany him on dangerous expeditions as well as travel on diplomatic missions. After

(continued on page 32)

(continued from page 31)

about 1505, however, Ariosto had begun working on *Orlando furioso*, and, indeed, he continued to revise and refine it for the rest of his life.

Orlando furioso is an original continuation of Matteo Boiardo's poem *Orlando innamorato.* Its hero is Orlando, whose name is the Italian form of Roland. *Orlando furioso* consists of a number of episodes derived from the epics, romances, and heroic poetry of the Middle Ages and Early Renaissance. The poem nevertheless achieves homogeneity by the author's skill and economy in handling the various episodes and by his ability to confer on his characters his own refined spirituality. Sensual love is the prevailing sentiment, but it is tempered by the author's ironical attitude and artistic detachment. Upon its publication in 1516, *Orlando furioso* enjoyed immediate popularity throughout Europe, and it was to influence greatly the literature of the Renaissance.

Ariosto's five comedies, *Cassaria* (1508), *I suppositi* (1509), *Il negromante* (1520), *La lena* (1529), and *I studenti* (completed by his brother Gabriele and published posthumously as *La scolastica*), are based on the Latin classics but were inspired by contemporary life. Though minor works in themselves, they were among the first of those imitations of Latin comedy in the vernacular that would long characterize European comedy.

her a picture of her own willfulness, Petruchio obliges her to forgo food, sleep, and fancy clothing. He abuses his own servants, notably Grumio, as a way of demonstrating how unattractive a sharp temper can be. Katharina learns, however reluctantly, that the only way she can find peace is to agree with anything that Petruchio says and do whatever he insists. At the play's end, Petruchio wins a bet from the other gentlemen that Katharina will be more obedient

Actress Janet McTeer (right), *as Petruchio, tries to tame Katherine Hunter's Katharina in an all-female production of* The Taming of the Shrew, *staged at the Globe Theatre in 2003.* Ferdaus Shamim/ WireImage/Getty Images

than their new wives. To show that she is indeed now more obedient, on Petruchio's orders Katharina delivers a short sermon on the virtues of wifely obedience.

The play's other plot follows the competition between Hortensio, Gremio, and Lucentio for Bianca's hand in marriage. The only serious candidate is Lucentio, the son of a wealthy Florentine gentleman. He is so smitten with Bianca's charms that he exchanges places with his clever servant, Tranio, in order to gain access to the woman he loves. He does so disguised as a tutor. So does the less-successful Hortensio. Gremio has nothing to recommend his suit except his wealth; he is an old man, unattractive to Bianca. In order to fend off this claim of wealth (since Baptista has vowed to bestow Bianca on the suitor with the greatest wealth), Tranio poses as the son of a wealthy gentleman and steps into the competition for Bianca's hand. Needing a father to prove his claim, Tranio persuades a pedant (or merchant) from Mantua to play the role. This ruse fools Baptista, and so the formal arrangements for the marriage proceed. Tranio's tricks are eventually exposed, but not before Lucentio and Bianca have taken the occasion to marry in secret. Hortensio, in the meantime, has forsaken his pursuit of Bianca and married a wealthy widow. In the play's final scene, both Bianca and Hortensio's new wife ironically prove to be shrewish.

Chapter 3

The Later Romantic Comedies

In the second half of the 1590s, Shakespeare brought to perfection the genre of romantic comedy that he had helped to invent. *A Midsummer Night's Dream*, one of the most successful of all his plays, displays the kind of multiple plotting he had practiced in *The Taming of the Shrew* and other earlier comedies. In it, he unites four separate strands or plots with one another. Despite the play's brevity, it is a masterpiece of artful construction.

A MIDSUMMER NIGHT'S DREAM

Shakespeare wrote this play about 1595–96, and it was published in 1600 in a quarto edition from the author's manuscript, in which there are some minor inconsistencies. The version published in the First Folio of 1623 was taken from a second quarto edition, with some reference to a promptbook. It is considered one of the "great" or "middle" comedies, and it has long been one of the most popular of Shakespeare's plays.

Theseus, duke of Athens, has conquered Hippolyta, the Amazon queen, and is about to wed her. Meanwhile, two lovers, Hermia and Lysander, seek refuge in the forest near Athens when Hermia's father demands that she marry Demetrius. Hoping to win Demetrius's favour, Helena tells him their whereabouts and follows him to the forest, where he goes in search of Hermia. The forest is also full of fairies who have come for the duke's wedding. Oberon, the king of the fairies, quarrels with his queen, Titania, and bids his mischievous servant Puck to drop magic juice into her eyes as she sleeps; his intent is to punish her for her disobedience by causing her to fall hopelessly in love with whatever person or creature she happens to see when she awakes. Noting that the human lovers in the forest are also at odds, he orders Puck to drop the love juice into Demetrius's eyes so that Demetrius's one-time affection for Helena will be restored. Because the two young Athenian men look much alike, however, Puck mistakenly administers the love juice to Lysander, who then happens to see Helena when he awakes. He falls hopelessly in love with her. Now both young men are in love with Helena and neither with the poor deserted Hermia. This situation

PUCK

In medieval English folklore, a puck was a malicious fairy or demon. In Old and Middle English the word meant simply "demon." In Elizabethan lore some malevolence was removed from the connotation, and a puck became a mischievous fairy much like a brownie (a small industrious fairy believed to inhabit houses and barns); this spirit was also called Robin Goodfellow, or Hobgoblin. As one of the leading characters in William Shakespeare's *A Midsummer Night's Dream,* Puck boasts of his pranks of changing shapes, misleading travelers at night, spoiling milk, frightening young girls, and tripping venerable old dames. The Irish pooka, or *púca*, and the Welsh *pwcca* are similar household spirits.

does not make Helena any happier, though. She comes to the conclusion that they are all making fun of her. Hermia and Helena fall out over this contretemps, while the young men have become fierce and even would-be murderous rivals of one another for Helena. All is at sixes and sevens.

In the same woods a group of artisans are rehearsing an entertainment for the duke's wedding. Ever playful, Puck gives one of the "mechanicals," Nick Bottom, an ass's head; when Titania awakens, she falls in love with Bottom. After much general confusion and comic misunderstanding, Oberon's magic restores Titania and the four lovers to their original states. The duke invites the two couples to join him and Hippolyta in a triple wedding. The wedding celebration features Bottom's troupe in a comically inept performance of their play, *The Most Lamentable Comedy and Most Cruel Death of Pyramus and Thisbe*, which turns out to be a parody of the perilous encounters the various lovers have experienced in the forest and somehow managed to survive.

The use of multiple plots encourages a varied treatment of the experiencing of love. For the two young human couples, falling in love is quite hazardous; the long-standing friendship between the two young women is threatened and almost destroyed by the rivalries of heterosexual encounter. The eventual transition to heterosexual marriage seems to them to have been a process of dreaming, indeed of nightmare, from which they emerge miraculously restored to their best selves. Meantime the marital strife of Oberon and Titania is, more disturbingly, one in which the female is humiliated until she submits to the will of her husband. Similarly, Hippolyta is an Amazon warrior queen who has had to submit to the authority of a husband. Fathers and daughters are no less at strife until, as in a dream, all is resolved by the magic of Puck and Oberon. Love is ambivalently both an enduring ideal

Actors portraying (left to right, foreground) *a transformed Bottom and the fairy queen Titania performing in* A Midsummer Night's Dream *during the Czech Republic's 2009 Summer Shakespeare Theatre Festival.* Isifa/FilmMagic/Getty Images

relationship and a struggle for mastery in which the male has the upper hand.

THE MERCHANT OF VENICE

Written about 1596–97, this play was printed in a quarto edition in 1600 from an authorial manuscript or copy of one. In it, Bassanio, a noble but penniless Venetian, asks his wealthy merchant friend Antonio for a loan so that Bassanio can undertake a journey to woo the heiress Portia.

Antonio, whose money is invested in foreign ventures, borrows the sum from Shylock, a Jewish moneylender, on the condition that, if the loan cannot be repaid in time, Antonio will forfeit a pound of flesh. Antonio is reluctant to do business with Shylock, whom he despises for lending money at interest (unlike Antonio himself, who provides the money for Bassanio without any such financial obligation); Antonio considers that lending at interest violates the very spirit of Christianity. Nevertheless, he needs help in order to be able to assist Bassanio. Meanwhile, Bassanio has met the terms of Portia's father's will by selecting from three caskets the one that contains her portrait, and he and Portia marry. (Two previous wooers, the princes of Monaco and Aragon, have failed the casket test by choosing what many men desire or what the chooser thinks he deserves. Bassanio knows that he must paradoxically "give and hazard all he hath" to win the lady.) News arrives that Antonio's ships have been lost at sea. Unable to collect on his loan, Shylock attempts to use justice to enforce a terrible, murderous revenge on Antonio: he demands his pound of flesh.

Shylock's desire for vengeance is motivated by the way in which the Christians of the play have banded together to enable his daughter Jessica to elope from his house, taking with her a substantial portion of his wealth, in order to become the bride of the Christian Lorenzo. Shylock's revengeful plan is foiled by Portia, disguised as a lawyer, who turns the tables on Shylock by a legal quibble: he must take flesh only, and Shylock must die if any blood is spilled. Thus, the contract is canceled, and Shylock is ordered to give half of his estate to Antonio, who agrees not to take the money if Shylock converts to Christianity and restores his disinherited daughter to his will. Shylock has little choice but to agree. The play ends with the news that, in fact, some of Antonio's ships have arrived safely.

Members of an Israeli theatre company rehearse a scene from a Hebrew-language version of The Merchant of Venice *at the Globe Theatre, May 2012.* Leon Neal/AFP/Getty Images

SHYLOCK

The character of Shylock, the Jewish moneylender in *The Merchant of Venice*, is a somewhat tragic figure. His role and Shakespeare's intentions have been the subject of much scholarly debate over whether the playwright displays anti-Semitism or religious tolerance in his characterization, for, despite his stereotypical usurious nature, Shylock is depicted as understandably full of hate, having been both verbally and physically abused by Christians and losing both his daughter and his wealth to a Christian. Shylock is given one of Shakespeare's most eloquent speeches:

> He hath disgraced me, and hindered me half a million, laughed at my losses, mocked at my gains, scorned my nation, thwarted my bargains, cooled my friends, heated mine enemies; and what's his reason? I am a Jew. Hath not a Jew eyes? Hath not a Jew hands, organs, dimensions, senses, affections, passions? Fed with the same food, hurt with the same weapons, subject to the same diseases, healed by the same means, warmed and cooled by the same winter and summer, as a Christian is? If you prick us, do we not bleed? If you tickle us, do we not laugh? If you poison us, do we not die? And if you wrong us, shall we not revenge? If we are like you in the rest, we will resemble you in that. If a Jew wrong a Christian, what is his humility? Revenge. If a Christian wrong a Jew, what should his sufferance be by Christian example? Why, revenge. The villainy you teach me I will execute, and it shall go hard but I will better the instruction. (Act 3, scene1)

Shakespeare's double plot structure contrasts a tale of romantic wooing with one that comes close to tragedy. Portia is a fine example of a romantic heroine in Shakespeare's mature comedies: she is witty, rich, exacting in what she expects of men, and adept at putting herself in a male disguise to make her presence felt. She is loyally obedient to her father's will and yet determined that she shall have Bassanio. She triumphantly resolves the murky legal affairs of Venice when the men have all failed. Portia foils Shylock in a way that is both clever and shystering. Ultimately she triumphs, not only with Shylock in the court of law but in her marriage with Bassanio.

MUCH ADO ABOUT NOTHING

This play was written probably in 1598–99 and printed in a quarto edition from the author's own manuscript in 1600. The play takes an ancient theme—that of a woman falsely accused of unfaithfulness—to brilliant comedic heights. Shakespeare used as his main source for the Claudio-Hero plot a story from Matteo Bandello's *Novelle* (1554–73). He also may have consulted Ludovico Ariosto's *Orlando furioso* and Edmund Spenser's *The Faerie Queene*. The Beatrice-Benedick plot is essentially Shakespeare's own, though he must have had in mind his own story of wife taming in *The Taming of the Shrew*.

Shakespeare sets up a contrast between the conventional Claudio and Hero, who have the usual expectations of each other, and Beatrice and Benedick, who are highly skeptical of romance and courtship and, seemingly, each other. Claudio is deceived by the jealous Don John into believing that Hero is prepared to abandon him for Claudio's friend and mentor, Don Pedro. This malicious fiction is soon dispelled, but Claudio seems not to have learned his lesson. He believes Don John a second time,

MATTEO BANDELLO

(b. 1485, Castelnuovo Scrivia, duchy of Milan [Italy]—d. 1561, Agen, France)

A monk, diplomat, and soldier as well as a writer, Bandello was educated at Milan and the University of Pavia. He frequented the courts of Ferrara and Mantua and knew statesman and writer Niccolò Machiavelli. The material for the book on which his reputation rests, *Novelle* ("Stories"), was destroyed in the Spanish attack on Milan (1522), and he fled to France. In 1550 he was made bishop of Agen and spent the remainder of his life in France writing.

Bandello's 214 tales were published in four volumes between 1554 and 1573. They are frequently daring or sensual in the manner of Giovanni Boccaccio's *Decameron*, and they provide valuable insights into the social intrigues of Renaissance Italy.

In the 1560s and '70s Bandello's stories were translated into both French and English, and the English translators took the liberty of adding a severe moral tone to the tales. The stories provided the themes for several important Elizabethan plays, notably Shakespeare's *Romeo and Juliet*, *Much Ado About Nothing*, and *Twelfth Night*, and John Webster's *The Duchess of Malfi*. Bandello started a new trend in 16th-century literature, and his influence can also be discerned in the literature of France and Spain, as well as that of England.

and on a much more serious charge—that Hero has had many lovers, that she is actually sleeping with another man, even on the night before her impending wedding to Claudio. Supported by Don Pedro, who also accepts the story (based on seeming visual evidence), Claudio publicly rejects Hero at the wedding ceremony. She is so shamed

Members of the Royal Shakespeare Company performing in a 2011 production of Much Ado About Nothing. © AP Images

that her family is obliged to report that she is dead. Don John's plot is eventually unveiled by the bumbling constable Dogberry and his comically inept fellow constable, but not before the story of Hero has taken a nearly tragic turn. Claudio's slanders of Hero have so outraged her cousin Beatrice that she turns to Benedick, pleading with him to kill Claudio. Former friends are near the point of mayhem until the revelations of the night watch prove the villainy of Don John and the innocence of Hero.

Meanwhile, Beatrice and Benedick carry on "a kind of merry war" that tests their wits in clever but crushing repartees. Both have a reputation for being scornful and wary of marriage. Though attracted to each other for many reasons, they find it virtually impossible to get beyond the game of one-upping each other. Eventually their friends have to intervene with a virtuous ruse designed to trick each of them into believing that the other is hopelessly but secretly suffering the pangs of love. The ruse works because it is essentially true. At the play's end, both couples are united.

This play could be regarded as a brilliant rewriting of *The Taming of the Shrew*. Its witty battle of the sexes is no less amusing and complicated than in the earlier play, but the eventual accommodation finds something much closer to mutual respect and equality between men and women.

AS YOU LIKE IT

Shakespeare based *As You Like It* on *Rosalynde* (1590), a prose romance by Thomas Lodge. Shakespeare's play was written and performed about 1598–1600 and first published in the First Folio of 1623.

The play has two principal settings: the court that Frederick has usurped from his brother, the rightful duke (known as Duke Senior), and the Forest of Arden, where the Duke and his followers (including the disgruntled Jaques) are living in exile. Rosalind, the Duke's daughter, who is still at court, falls in love with Orlando, who has been denied by his older brother Oliver the education and upbringing that should have been Orlando's right as a gentleman. To escape Oliver's murderous hatred, Orlando flees to the Forest of Arden with his faithful old servant Adam. Soon Rosalind is banished, too, merely for being the daughter of the out-of-favour Duke Senior. She flees to Arden dressed in male disguise for safety, accompanied by her cousin Celia and the jester Touchstone.

Disguised as "Ganymede," Rosalind encounters Orlando, lovesick for his Rosalind, and promises to cure

THOMAS LODGE

(b. *c.* 1557, London?, Eng.—d. 1625, London)

Thomas Lodge was the son of Sir Thomas Lodge, who was lord mayor of London in 1562. The younger Lodge was educated at Merchant Taylors' School and at Trinity College, Oxford, and he studied law at Lincoln's Inn, London, in 1578. Lodge's earliest work was an anonymous pamphlet (*c.* 1579) in reply to Stephen Gosson's attack on stage plays. He engaged in varied literary activity for a number of years. His *Scillaes Metamorphosis* (1589), an Ovidian verse fable, is one of the earliest English poems to retell a classical story with imaginative embellishments, and it strongly influenced Shakespeare's *Venus and Adonis*. Lodge's *Phillis* (1593) contains amorous sonnets and pastoral eclogues from French and Italian originals. In *A Fig for Momus* (1595), he introduced classical satires and verse epistles (modeled after those of Juvenal and Horace) into English literature for the first time. His *Rosalynde: Euphues Golden Legacie* (1590) provided the plot for Shakespeare's comedy. His other romances are chiefly notable for the fine lyric poems scattered through them. In 1594 Lodge published two plays, *The Wounds of Civil War* and (with Robert Greene) *A Looking Glasse for London and England*.

To escape poverty Lodge took part in unprofitable freebooting voyages to the Canary Islands in 1588 and to South America in 1591. In 1597 he became a Roman Catholic, and he graduated in medicine from the University of Avignon in 1598. He received another M.D. degree from Oxford in 1602. Thereafter he practiced medicine in London and in Brussels, where he took refuge as a recusant following exposure of the Gunpowder Plot (1605), the conspiracy of English Roman Catholics to blow up Parliament and King James I. Lodge was back in England by 1612, became a distinguished physician in London, and died there while fighting the plague in 1625. His later works include *A Treatise of the Plague* (1603) and two major translations: *The Works of Lucius Annaeus Seneca* (1614) and *The Famous and Memorable Works of Josephus* (1620), both of which went through many editions.

him of his lovesickness by pretending to be that very Rosalind, so that Orlando will learn something of what women are really like. "Ganymede" befriends Orlando, offering him counseling in the affairs of love. Orlando, much in need of such advice, readily accepts and proceeds to woo his "Rosalind" ("Ganymede" playing her own self) as though she were indeed a woman. Her wryly amusing perspectives on the follies of young love helpfully puncture Orlando's inflated and unrealistic "Petrarchan" stance as the young lover who writes poems to his mistress and sticks them up on trees. Once he has learned that love is not a fantasy of invented attitudes, Orlando is ready to be the husband of the real young woman (actually played by a boy actor, of course), who is presented to him as the transformed Ganymede-Rosalind.

Oliver appears in the forest intending to kill Orlando, but, when Orlando saves his brother from a hungry lioness and a snake, Oliver experiences deep remorse. He then falls in love with Celia. Other figures in the play further an understanding of love's glorious foolishness by their various attitudes: Silvius, the pale-faced wooer out of pastoral romance; Phoebe, the disdainful mistress whom he worships; William, the country bumpkin, and Audrey, the country wench; and, surveying and commenting on every imaginable kind of human folly, the clown Touchstone and the malcontent traveler Jaques. Revelation of the girls' true identities precipitates a group wedding ceremony. When word arrives that Frederick has repented, the Duke's exile is at an end.

TWELFTH NIGHT

Twelfth Night; or, What You Will was written about 1600–02 and printed in the First Folio of 1623 from a transcript of an authorial draft or possibly a playbook. One of Shakespeare's finest comedies, the play precedes the great tragedies and problem plays in order of composition. Its original source appears to have been the story *Apollonius and Silla* in Barnabe Riche's *Riche His Farewell to Military Profession* (1581), based in turn on a number of Continental versions that included an Italian comedy called *Gl'ingannati* (1531; "The Deceived"), published anonymously, and a story in Bandello's *Novelle* (1554–73).

Like *As You Like It*, *Twelfth Night* pursues a motif of female disguise. Viola, cast ashore in Illyria by a shipwreck and separated from her twin brother Sebastian, whom she believes to have died in the event, is obliged to disguise herself as a young man, "Cesario," in order to gain a place in the court of Duke Orsino. She promptly falls in love with the duke. Orsino, who thinks he is in love with the lady Olivia, sends "Cesario" to plead his cause to Olivia, who promptly falls in love with the messenger.

As events play out, "Cesario" uses her disguise as a cover for an educational process not unlike that given by Rosalind to Orlando in *As You Like It*. Orsino is as unrealistic a lover as one could hope to imagine; he pays fruitless court to Olivia and seems content with the unproductive love melancholy in which he wallows. Only "Cesario" is able to awaken in him a genuine feeling for friendship and love. They become inseparable companions and then seeming rivals for the hand of Olivia until Shakespeare's stage magic restores "Cesario" to her woman's garments

Anne Hathaway and Raúl Esparza as an undisguised Viola and the object of her affection, Duke Orsino, in Shakespeare's Twelfth Night, *New York City, 2009.* Dimitrios Kambouris/WireImage/Getty Images

and thus presents to Orsino the flesh-and-blood woman whom he has only distantly imagined. (And, luckily for Olivia, Viola's twin appears on the scene, unscathed after all.) The transition from same-sex friendship to heterosexual union is a constant in Shakespearean comedy. Women are self-knowing, constant, and loyal; the men must learn a lot from the women.

As in the other plays as well, *Twelfth Night* neatly plays off this courtship theme with a second plot, here

CROSS-DRESSING IN SHAKESPEARE

Although Shakespeare's plays contain many warmly positive depictions of heterosexuality, Shakespeare is astute in his representations of sexual ambiguity. Viola—in disguise as a young man, "Cesario," in *Twelfth Night*—wins the love of Duke Orsino in such a delicate way that what appears to be the love between two men morphs into the heterosexual mating of Orsino and Viola. The ambiguity is reinforced by the audience's knowledge that in Shakespeare's theatre "Cesario"-Viola was portrayed by a boy actor of perhaps 16. All the cross-dressing situations in the comedies, involving Portia in *The Merchant of Venice*, "Ganymede"-Rosalind in *As You Like It*, Imogen in *Cymbeline*, and many others, playfully explore the uncertain boundaries between the genders. Rosalind's male disguise name in *As You Like It*, Ganymede, is that of the young male cupbearer to Zeus with whom the god was enamoured. The ancient legends assume that Ganymede was Zeus's lover. Shakespeare is characteristically delicate on that score, but he does seem to delight in the frisson of sexual suggestion.

involving the members of Olivia's household—Feste the jester, Maria, Olivia's uncle Sir Toby Belch, and Sir Toby's friend Sir Andrew Aguecheek. These individuals conspire to undermine the high-minded apostle of sobriety and decorum, Malvolio, by exposure and humiliation. They plant a love letter purportedly written by Olivia to Malvolio urging him to show his affection for her by smiling constantly and dressing himself in cross-garters and yellow. Malvolio is thoroughly discomfited and even locked up for a time as a supposed madman. His animosity toward merriment is a challenge not only to the merrymakers but to the play's more serious characters as well;

all must learn to embrace life's joys before those joys are overtaken by aging and death. At the play's end, Malvolio is the only solitary figure among the pairs of happy lovers.

THE MERRY WIVES OF WINDSOR

Shakespeare wrote *The Merry Wives of Windsor* sometime between 1597 and 1601 (probably near the earlier of these dates). The play centres on the comic romantic misadventures of Falstaff. *The Merry Wives of Windsor* was published in a quarto edition in 1602 from a reported and abbreviated text. The First Folio version of 1623 is from a transcript by

Falstaff as Herne the Hunter sitting between the titular wives during a rehearsal of The Broad Stage's 2010 production of The Merry Wives of Windsor, *in Santa Monica, Calif.* Amy Graves/WireImage/Getty Images

Ralph Crane (scrivener of the King's Men) of an authorial manuscript.

Although it contains elements of Plautus's comedies and Italian novelle, *The Merry Wives of Windsor* does not have a known source. The play differs from Shakespeare's other comedies of this period in that it is set not in an imaginary country but in Windsor, a solidly bourgeois village near Windsor Castle in the heart of England. There is little, however, in the way of romantic wooing (the story of Anne Page and her suitor Fenton is rather buried in the midst of so many other goings-on), but the play's portrayal of women, and especially of the two "merry wives," Mistress Alice Ford and Mistress Margaret Page, reaffirms what is so often true of women in these early plays, that they are good-hearted, chastely loyal, and wittily self-possessed. Falstaff, a suitable butt for their cleverness, is a scapegoat figure who must be publicly humiliated as a way of transferring onto him the human frailties that Windsor society wishes to expunge.

Shakespeare's ploy in this engaging comedy is to introduce Falstaff, already a household name in London in the late 1590s, into a nonhistorical plot where he occupies a very different role from that of Shakespeare's earlier *Henry IV* history plays. (Uncertain tradition has it that Queen Elizabeth wanted to see Falstaff in love.) Along with Falstaff, Shakespeare also imports some other characters who appear in the *Henry IV* plays, such as Pistol, Bardolph, Nym, Mistress Quickly, and Justice Shallow. They are all in a delightfully new environment.

Falstaff takes a fancy to two married women, Mistress Page and Mistress Ford, who are said to control their own financial affairs and thus to be moderately wealthy. He writes identical love letters to them, hoping to swindle some money from them while also enjoying them as sexual partners. He tries to engage the assistance of Pistol and

HERNE THE HUNTER

In *Merry Wives*, Falstaff disguises himself as Herne the Hunter, a phantom hunter who haunts Windsor Great Park. Though Herne may have been an actual keeper of the forest, he is probably a local manifestation of the Wild Huntsman myth known throughout the world. The usual story associated with the Wild Hunt involves someone excessively fond of the chase who makes a rash pledge or compact with a stranger (the devil) and is thus doomed to hunt forever. Herne is said to ride at night, especially during storms. He wears horns, rattles chains, blasts trees and cattle, and occasionally appears to mortals.

Nym but is scorned by them. When he discharges them from his service, they go off and inform the husbands of Mistresses Page and Ford of Falstaff's plot. The wives compare their letters and resolve to trick the "greasy knight." Twice the wives fool Falstaff, and this results in his being dumped in a muddy ditch and, later, disguised as a witch and beaten. The trickery of the two women also serves to frustrate the jealous behaviour of Master Ford. Mistress Ford lets her husband in on the joke at last, and the two couples, Pages and Fords, happily plan one more ruse at Falstaff's expense.

A secondary plot centres on the wooing of the Pages' charming daughter Anne. Doctor Caius, Slender, and Fenton are rivals for Anne's affection. To great comic effect, all three suitors use Caius's servant Mistress Quickly to argue their case to young Anne. Slender is favoured by Master Page, who devises a plan for Slender and Anne to elope after the play's climactic scene. Mistress Page, who favours Caius as a son-in-law, devises a similar plan.

In the climactic scene, set in Windsor Forest, Falstaff dresses himself absurdly as Herne the Hunter, complete with stag's horns, expecting an assignation. The women and their husbands, however, have arranged for a group of friends, including Anne Page, in witch and fairy costumes, to frighten and tease him. The marriage plans conceived by Master and Mistress Page are foiled when Anne elopes with Fenton, the suitor of her choice. All identities are revealed at the end, and, in an atmosphere of good humour, Fenton is welcomed into the Page family and Falstaff is forgiven.

Chapter 4

Shakespeare's Other Comedies and Romances

Whatever his reasons, about 1599–1600 Shakespeare turned with unsparing intensity to the exploration of darker issues such as revenge, sexual jealousy, aging, midlife crisis, and death. Perhaps he saw that his own life was moving into a new phase of more complex and vexing experiences. Perhaps he felt, or sensed, that he had worked through the romantic comedy and history play and the emotional trajectories of maturation that they encompassed. At any event, he began writing not only his great tragedies but a group of plays that are hard to classify in terms of genre. They are sometimes grouped today as "problem" plays or "problem" comedies. *All's Well That Ends Well* and *Measure for Measure* are two of the three so-called problem plays, and an examination of these plays is crucial to understanding this period of transition from 1599 to 1605.

Concurrently with his great tragedies, and then in the years that followed, Shakespeare turned again to the writing of comedy. The late comedies are usually called romances or tragicomedies because they tell stories of wandering and separation leading eventually to tearful and joyous reunion. They are suffused with a bittersweet mood that seems eloquently appropriate to a writer whose tragedies explored with such unsparing honesty the depths of human suffering and degradation.

ALL'S WELL THAT ENDS WELL

Shakespeare wrote this comedy in 1601–05, and it was published in the First Folio of 1623 seemingly from a theatrical playbook that still retained certain authorial features or from a literary transcript either of the playbook or of an authorial manuscript. The principal source of the plot was a tale in Giovanni Boccaccio's *Decameron*.

The play concerns the efforts of Helena, daughter of a renowned physician to the recently deceased count of Rossillion, to win as her husband the young new count, Bertram. When Bertram leaves Rossillion to become a courtier, Helena follows after, hoping to minister to the gravely ill king of France with a miraculous cure that her father had bequeathed to her. In return for her success in doing so, the king invites her to select a husband, her choice being Bertram. The young man, unwilling to marry so far below himself in social station, accedes to the royal imperative but promptly flees to military action in Tuscany with his vapid but engaging friend Parolles. By letter Bertram informs Helena that he may not be considered her husband until she has taken the ring from his finger and conceived a child by him.

Disguised as a pilgrim, Helena follows Bertram to Florence only to discover that he has been courting Diana, the daughter of her hostess. Helena spreads a rumour of her own death and arranges a nighttime rendezvous with Bertram in which she substitutes herself for Diana. In exchange for his ring, she gives him one that the king has given her. When Bertram returns to Rossillion, where the king is visiting the countess, the royal guest recognizes the ring and suspects foul play. Helena then appears to explain her machinations and claim her rightful spouse.

THE "BED TRICK"

Of Shakespeare's three "problem" plays dating from 1599–1605—*All's Well That Ends Well*, *Measure for Measure*, and *Troilus and Cressida*—two incorporate the so-called bed trick as an important plot device. *All's Well* is a comedy ending in acceptance of marriage, but in a way that poses thorny ethical issues. Count Bertram cannot initially accept his marriage to Helena, a woman of lower social station who has grown up in his noble household and has won Bertram as her husband by her seemingly miraculous cure of the French king. Bertram's reluctance to face the responsibilities of marriage is all the more dismaying when he turns his amorous intentions to a Florentine maiden, Diana, whom he wishes to seduce without marriage. Helena's stratagem to resolve this difficulty is the so-called bed trick, substituting herself in Bertram's bed for the arranged assignation and then calling her wayward husband to account when she is pregnant with his child. Her ends are achieved by such morally ambiguous means that marriage seems at best a precarious institution on which to base the presumed reassurances of romantic comedy. The pathway toward resolution and emotional maturity is not easy. Helena proves to be a more ambiguous heroine than Rosalind or Viola.

Measure for Measure similarly employs the bed trick, and for a similar purpose, though in even murkier circumstances. Isabella, on the verge of becoming a nun, learns that she has attracted the sexual desire of Lord Angelo, the deputy ruler of Vienna serving in the mysterious absence of the Duke. Her plea to Angelo for her brother's life, when that brother (Claudio) has been sentenced to die for fornication with his fiancée, is met with a demand that she agree to have sex with Angelo or forfeit Claudio's life. This ethical dilemma is resolved by a trick (devised by the Duke, in disguise) to substitute for Isabella a

(continued on page 58)

(continued from page 57)

woman (Mariana) whom Angelo was supposed to marry but refused when she could produce no dowry. As in *All's Well*, the bed trick in *Measure for Measure* achieves a (mostly) happy ending through morally dubious means.

MEASURE FOR MEASURE

Shakespeare wrote this "dark" comedy about 1603–04, and it was published in the First Folio of 1623 from a transcript of an authorial draft. The play examines the complex interplay of mercy and justice. Shakespeare adapted the story from *Epitia*, a tragedy by Italian dramatist Giambattista Giraldi, and especially from a two-part play by George Whetstone titled *Promos and Cassandra* (1578).

The play opens with Vincentio, the benevolent duke of Vienna, commissioning his deputy Angelo to govern the city while he travels to Poland. In actuality, the Duke remains in Vienna disguised as a friar in order to watch what unfolds. Following the letter of the law, Angelo passes the death sentence on Claudio, a nobleman convicted for impregnating his betrothed, Juliet. Claudio's sister Isabella, a novice in a nunnery, pleads his case to Angelo. This new deputy ruler, a man of stern and rigorous self-control, finds to his consternation and amazement that he lusts after Isabella. Her virgin purity awakens in him a desire that more profligate sexual opportunities could not. Hating himself for doing so, he offers to spare Claudio's life if Isabella will have sex with him. She refuses and is further outraged when her brother begs her to reconsider.

On the advice of the disguised Vincentio, Isabella schedules the rendezvous with Angelo, but secretly arranges for her place to be taken by Mariana, the woman

GIAMBATTISTA GIRALDI

(b. 1504, Ferrara [Italy]—d. Dec. 30, 1573, Ferrara)

Also called Cynthius, or Cinthio (Italian Cinzio), Giraldi was influenced by the revival of Aristotelian literary principles after the publication in Latin of the original text of Aristotle's *Poetics* in 1536. In his poem *Ercole* (1557; "Hercules") he tried to reconcile the Aristotelian rules with modern taste. In his *Discorso delle comedie e delle tragedie* (1543; "Discourse on Comedy and Tragedy") he reacted against the austerity of the classical tragedies. In his own tragedies—*Orbecche* (1541), his only strictly Senecan tragedy; *Didone* (1542); *Altile* (1543); *Cleopatra* (1543); *Selene; Eufimia; Arrenopia; Epitia,* from which Shakespeare's *Measure for Measure* derives; and *Antivalomeni* (1549)—he included new dramatic elements while conforming to the Aristotelian rules.

Writing for a popular audience, he supplied the requisite horror and violence, but he altered the Senecan model to provide a happy ending, thus producing some of the first tragicomedies. Giraldi's *Ecatommiti* (1565), which collected 112 stories in the manner of Boccaccio's *Decameron*, aimed at stylistic distinction and, in the manner of Matteo Bandello, showed an appreciation for direct narrative. Shakespeare's *Othello* derives from Giraldi's story of the Moor of Venice.

Angelo was once engaged to marry but whom he then disavowed because her dowry had been lost. Afterward, Angelo reneges on his promise to save Claudio, fearing that the young man knows too much and is therefore dangerous. Vincentio, reemerging at last from his supposed journey, presides over a finale in which Angelo is discredited

Actor Liam Brennan as Angelo attempts to woo a reluctant Isabella (Sophie Thompson) in a 2004 production of Measure for Measure *at the Globe Theatre.* Elliot Franks/WireImage/Getty Images

and ordered to marry Mariana. Claudio, having been saved from execution by the secret substitution of one who has died in prison, is allowed to marry Juliet. Lucio, an engaging but irresponsible woman chaser and scandalmonger, is reproved by Vincentio and obliged to marry a prostitute with whom he has had a child. The rascally underworld figures (the bawd Mistress Overdone, her pimp Pompey, and her customer Froth) who have exploited the sexual freedom of Vienna despite the wonderfully inept policing attempts of Constable Elbow are finally brought to justice, partly through the careful supervision of the magistrate Escalus. Vincentio asks Isabella to give up her idea of being a nun in order to become his wife. (Whether she accepts is today a matter of theatrical choice.)

Much about the play is thought-provoking. The Duke's motivations in manipulating all of the play's substitutions and false appearances are unclear, though arguably his wish is to see what the various characters of this play will do when faced with seemingly impossible choices. Angelo is revealed as a morally fallen man, a would-be seducer and murderer who is nonetheless remorseful and ultimately glad to have been prevented from carrying out his intended crimes. Claudio learns that he is coward enough to wish to live by any means, including the emotional and physical blackmail of his sister. Isabella learns that she is capable of bitterness and hatred, even if, crucially, she finally discovers that she can and must forgive her enemy. Her charity, and the Duke's stratagems, make possible an ending in forgiveness and marriage, but in that process the nature and meaning of marriage are severely tested.

PERICLES

This play was written about 1606–08 and published in a quarto edition in 1609, a defective and at times nearly unintelligible text that shows signs of having been memorially reconstructed. The editors of the First Folio of 1623 did not include *Pericles* in that edition, which suggests that they did not think it to be all or substantially by Shakespeare. The play was based on the Classical tale of Apollonius of Tyre as told in Book VIII of *Confessio amantis* by John Gower and in *The Pattern of Painful Adventures* by Laurence Twine.

The spirit of Gower opens the play and sets the stage with the title character in Antioch seeking to marry the princess. Pericles, however, discovers the truth about King Antiochus's incestuous love for his own daughter and flees, leaving the loyal Helicanus to rule Tyre in his absence. After aiding the starving people of Tarsus, Pericles is shipwrecked near Pentapolis, where he wins the hand of the beautiful Thaisa, daughter of King Simonides. As the couple sail back to Tyre, Thaisa gives birth to Marina during a violent storm. Pericles, believing his wife has died in childbirth, buries her at sea, but she is rescued and joins the temple of the goddess Diana at Ephesus. Pericles leaves his newborn daughter with Cleon, the governor of Tarsus, and his wife, Dionyza.

Marina, grown to young womanhood, is hated by Dionyza, who orders her murder. Instead, she is kidnapped by pirates and sold to a brothel, where she earns her keep by singing and doing needlework. Marina is reunited with her father when he is brought to her, mute and sick from years of grief. Pericles then has a vision of Diana, who sends them to Ephesus to be reunited with Thaisa.

The play is episodic, highly symbolic, and filled with imagery of the stormy seas. The most significant recurring theme is the proper relationship between parent and child, especially between father and daughter. Shakespeare returned to this theme often in his other late plays.

JOHN GOWER

(b. 1330?—d. 1408, London?)

Gower, a medieval English poet, wrote in the tradition of courtly love and moral allegory. His reputation once matched that of his contemporary and friend Geoffrey Chaucer, and he strongly influenced the writing of the other poets of his day. It is thought from Gower's language that he was of Kentish origin, though his family may have come from Yorkshire, and he was clearly a man of some wealth. Allusions in his poetry and other documents, however, indicate that he knew London well and was probably a court official. At one point, he professed acquaintance with Richard II, and in 1399 he was granted two pipes (casks) of wine a year for life by Henry IV as a reward for complimentary references in one of his poems. In 1397, living as a layman in the priory of St. Mary Overie, Southwark, London, Gower married Agnes Groundolf, who survived him. In 1400 Gower described himself as "senex et cecus" ("old and blind"), and on Oct. 24, 1408, his will was proved; he left bequests to the Southwark priory, where he is buried.

Gower's three major works are in French, English, and Latin, and he also wrote a series of French balades intended for the English court. The *Speculum meditantis*, or *Mirour de l'omme*, in French, is composed of 12-line stanzas. Gower's major Latin poem, the *Vox clamantis*, owes much to Ovid. Gower's English poems include *In Praise of Peace*, in which he pleads urgently with the king to avoid the horrors of war, but his greatest English work is the *Confessio amantis*, essentially a collection of exemplary tales of love, whereby Venus's priest, Genius, instructs the poet, Amans, in the art of both courtly and Christian love. The stories are chiefly adapted from classical and medieval sources and are told with a tenderness and the restrained narrative art that constitute Gower's main appeal today.

The story is typical romance. Shakespeare adds touching scenes of reunion and a perception that beneath the naive account of travel lies a subtle dramatization of separation, loss, and recovery. Pericles is deeply burdened by his loss and perhaps, too, guilt-ridden for having consented to consign his wife's body to the sea. He is recovered from his despair only by the ministrations of a loving daughter, who is able to give him a reason to live again and then to be reunited with his wife.

THE WINTER'S TALE

This play, written about 1609–11, was published in the First Folio of 1623 from a transcript, by scrivener Ralph Crane, of an authorial manuscript or possibly the playbook. One of Shakespeare's final plays, *The Winter's Tale* is a romantic comedy with elements of tragedy.

The plot was based on a work of prose fiction called *Pandosto* (1588) by Robert Greene. The play opens with Leontes, the king of Sicilia, entertaining his old friend Polixenes, the king of Bohemia. Leontes jealously mistakes the courtesy between his wife, Hermione, and Polixenes as a sign of Hermione's adultery with him. In a fit of jealousy, he attempts to have Polixenes killed, but Polixenes escapes with Camillo, Leontes's faithful counselor, whom Leontes has sent to kill him. The pregnant Hermione is then publicly humiliated and thrown in jail, despite her protests of innocence. When the child, a girl, is born, Leontes rejects the child out of hand and gives her over to Antigonus, the husband of Hermione's attendant Paulina. Antigonus is instructed to abandon the baby in some wild place. Having learned of his mother's mistreatment, Leontes's beloved son Mamillius dies, and Hermione, too, is carried out and reported dead. Having

ROBERT GREENE

(b. July 1558?, Norwich, Eng.—d. Sept. 3, 1592, London)

Greene obtained degrees at both Cambridge and Oxford. He then went to London, where he became an intimate of its underworld. He wrote more than 35 works between 1580 and 1592. To be certain of supplying material attractive to the public, Greene at first slavishly followed literary fashions. His first model was John Lyly's *Euphues*.

In the later 1580s Greene wrote prose pastorals in the manner of Sir Philip Sidney's *Arcadia*, interspersed with charming, often irrelevant lyrics that have given Greene a reputation as a poet. The best of his pastorals is *Pandosto* (1588), the direct source of Shakespeare's *The Winter's Tale*.

About 1590 Greene began to compose serious didactic works. Beginning with *Greenes Never Too Late* (1590), he related prodigal son stories. That Greene drew on his own experience is evident from the tract *Greenes Groatsworth of Wit, Bought with a Million of Repentance*, printed posthumously in 1592 with Greene's admission that the experiences of the character that is its primary focus, Roberto, were essentially his own. In *Groatsworth* appears the first printed reference to Shakespeare, assailed as "an upstart Crow, beautified with our feathers, that with his *Tygers heart wrapt in a Players hide*, supposes he is as well able to bumbast out a blanke verse as the best of you ... in his owne conceit the onely Shake-scene in a countrie." (The words in italics are from Shakespeare's *Henry VI, Part 1*.) Greene is thought to be criticizing Shakespeare the actor.

Greene's writings for the theatre present numerous problems; the dating of his plays is conjectural, and his role as collaborator has produced much inconclusive discussion. With *The Honorable History of Friar Bacon and Friar Bungay*

(continued on page 66)

(continued from page 65)

(written *c.* 1591, published 1594), the first successful romantic comedy in English, Greene realized his comic talent in drama. In *The Scottish History of James the Fourth, Slaine at Flodden* (written *c.* 1590, published 1598) he used an Italian tale but drew on fairy lore for the characters of Oberon and Bohan. It was a forerunner of *As You Like It* and *A Midsummer Night's Dream*. As Christopher Marlowe anticipated the tragedies of Shakespeare, so, in a lesser way, Greene furnished him a model in dramatic comedy and romance.

lost everyone important to him and having realized the error of his ways, Leontes is left to his solitary despair.

Meanwhile, the baby girl, named Perdita, is brought up by a shepherd and his wife in Polixenes's kingdom of Bohemia. She appears in Act IV as a young and beautiful shepherdess who has been discovered by Polixenes's son Florizel. Needless to say, her true status is eventually discovered once she and Florizel have arrived at Leontes's court in Sicilia. In a climactic ending, Hermione is discovered to be alive after all. She had been sequestered by Paulina for some 16 years until the time for reunion and reconciliation arrived. Leontes is shown a seeming statue of Hermione, so lifelike that one might imagine it breathes. The "statue" comes to life, and Hermione is seen to have aged during her years of separation and waiting. Leontes, to his intense joy, realizes that he loves his wife more than ever. The recovery of the daughter he attempted to kill is no less precious to him. All is forgiven.

In certain respects, *The Winter's Tale* is a replaying of elements of *Pericles*, in that Leontes brings about the seeming death of that wife and the real death of their

The shepherdess-cum-princess Perdita being wooed by Prince Florizel in a 2011 production of The Winter's Tale by the Royal Shakespeare Company, in New York City.© AP Images

son. The resulting guilt is unbearable for Leontes and yet ultimately curative over a period of many years that are required for his daughter to grow to maturity apart from him. The reunion with daughter and then wife is deeply touching as in *Pericles*, with the added magical touch that the audience does not know that Hermione is alive and in fact has been told that she is dead. Her wonderfully staged appearance as a statue coming to life is one of the great theatrical coups in Shakespeare, playing as it does with favourite Shakespearean themes in these late plays of the ministering daughter, the guilt-ridden husband, and the miraculously recovered wife. The story is all the more moving when one considers that Shakespeare may have had, or imagined, a similar experience of attempting to recover a relationship with his wife, Anne, whom he had left in Stratford during his many years in London.

CYMBELINE

This play was written in 1608–10 and published in the First Folio of 1623 from a careful transcript of an authorial manuscript incorporating a theatrical playbook that had included many authorial stage directions. Set in the pre-Christian Roman world, *Cymbeline* draws its main theme, that of a wager by a husband on his wife's fidelity, from a story in Boccaccio's *Decameron*.

Disguised as a boy, Imogen is taken in by Belarius (left) *and her kidnapped brothers in a scene from* Cymbeline *at London's Barbican Theatre, 2007.* Elliot Franks/WireImage/Getty Images

THE *DECAMERON*

It was probably in the years 1348–53 that Boccaccio composed the *Decameron* in the form in which it is read today. In the broad sweep of its range and its alternately tragic and comic views of life, it is rightly regarded as his masterpiece. Stylistically, it is the most perfect example of Italian classical prose, and its influence on Renaissance literature throughout Europe was enormous.

The *Decameron* begins with the flight of 10 young people (7 women and 3 men) from plague-stricken Florence in 1348. They retire to a rich, well-watered countryside, where, over the course of two weeks, each member of the party has a turn deciding in detail how their day shall be spent and, above all, the subject of their alternate storytelling. This storytelling occupies 10 days of the fortnight (the rest being set aside for personal adornment or for religious devotions); hence the title of the book itself, *Decameron*, or "Ten Days' Work." The stories thus amount to 100 in all. In addition to the 100 stories, Boccaccio has a master theme, namely, the way of life of the refined bourgeoisie, who combined respect for conventions with an open-minded attitude to personal behaviour.

The sombre tones of the opening passages of the book, in which the plague and the moral and social chaos that accompanies it are described in the grand manner, are in sharp contrast to the scintillating liveliness of Day I, which is spent almost entirely in witty disputation, and to the playful atmosphere of intrigue that characterizes the tales of adventure or deception related on Days II and III. With Day IV and its stories of unhappy love, the gloomy note returns; but Day V brings some relief, though it does not entirely dissipate the echo of solemnity, by giving happy endings to stories of love that does not at first run smoothly. Day VI reintroduces the gaiety of Day

(continued on page 70)

(continued from page 69)

I and constitutes the overture to the great comic score, Days VII, VIII, and IX, which are given over to laughter, trickery, and license. Finally, in Day X, all the themes of the preceding days are brought to a high pitch, the impure made pure and the common made heroic. In this work Boccaccio proved himself a master of the spoken word and of the swift, vivid, tense narrative free from the proliferation of ornament. The *Decameron* became the fountainhead of Italian literary prose for centuries to come.

In the play *Cymbeline*, the king of Britain, decides that his daughter, Imogen, must marry his witless and lecherous stepson Cloten. When Cymbeline learns that Imogen is secretly married to Posthumus Leonatus, he banishes Posthumus, who heads for Rome. In a conversation with a villainous Italian, Iachimo, Posthumus finds himself drawn unwisely into betting Iachimo that Imogen's fidelity to her marriage is unassailable. Journeying to England, Iachimo furtively obtains from the sleeping Imogen a token that he uses to convince Posthumus of her infidelity. Posthumus sends a servant to kill Imogen, but the servant instead warns her of the plan and she flees.

Disguising herself as a young boy (Fidele), Imogen sets out for Rome but loses her way in Wales. There she encounters Belarius and her two brothers, whom she had believed dead (Belarius had kidnapped Cymbeline's sons in retribution for his unjust banishment). Posthumus (who has left Rome), Imogen, and her brothers are caught up in the advance of the Roman army, which has come to collect the tribute that Cymbeline has refused to pay to Rome. The forces clash, and Cymbeline's army is victorious, largely because of the valour of Posthumus, Cymbeline's sons, and Belarius. A lengthy series of revelations and explanations ensue. Posthumus and Imogen are reunited. Cymbeline's now-dead queen is revealed to have been thoroughly wicked. Her son Cloten has died at the hands of one of Cymbeline's sons. And Cymbeline is reconciled to all his beleaguered family and to Belarius as well.

Cymbeline bears echoes of many other Shakespeare plays. Innocence and fidelity are questioned here as elsewhere. Particularly noteworthy is the portrayal of Cymbeline's baleful wife, a stereotypically wicked stepmother. She illustrates how ambivalent is Shakespeare's view of the mother in his late plays. She can be readily compared to Dionyza in *Pericles*. In her relentless desire for control, she also brings to mind Lady Macbeth and the Weird Sisters in *Macbeth*, as well as Coriolanus's mother, Volumnia. The devouring mother is a forbidding presence in the late plays, though she is counterbalanced by such redeeming maternal figures such as Hermione in *The Winter's Tale* and Thaisa in *Pericles*.

THE TEMPEST

This play was first written and performed about 1611 and published in the First Folio of 1623 from an edited transcript, by Crane, of the author's papers after they had been annotated for production.

The play opens with a storm raised by Prospero, who years earlier, as the rightful duke of Milan, had been set adrift in a boat with his three-year-old daughter, Miranda, by his usurping brother, Antonio. Prospero, more interested in his books and his magic than in the pragmatics of ruling Milan, had left himself vulnerable to this overthrow. Arriving at an island, Prospero had proceeded to make good use of his magic by freeing the sprite Ariel from the torment of imprisonment to which he had been subjected for refusing to carry out the wicked behests of the sorceress Sycorax. Prospero and Miranda had found no living person on the island other than Sycorax's son, Caliban. They had taken Caliban into their little family and lived in harmony until Caliban had attempted to rape Miranda. Prospero then had confined Caliban to a rock and to the status of slave, requiring him to attend to their needs by performing such tasks as gathering firewood.

As the play begins, Prospero raises the tempest in order to cast onto the shores of his island a party of Neapolitans returning to Naples from a wedding in Tunis: King Alonso of Naples, his son Ferdinand, his brother

A Canadian theatre troupe performing an adaptation of Shakespeare's The Tempest *at the 2008 Ibero-American Theatre Festival in Bogotá, Columbia.* Rodrigo Arangua/AFP/Getty Images

MAGIC IN LATE MEDIEVAL AND EARLY MODERN EUROPE

By the late Middle Ages (*c.* 1350–1450) and into the early modern period (*c.* 1450–1750), magic was regarded as part of a widespread and dangerously antisocial demonic cult that included the condemned practices of sorcery, necromancy, and witchcraft. Accused heretics, witches, and magicians were subject to inquisitions designed to uncover these cult connections and to destroy the means of transmission (e.g., the burning of condemned books and/or the "guilty" parties). The influential manual *Malleus maleficarum* (1486; "The Hammer of Witches") by Jacob Sprenger and Henry Krämer describes witchcraft in great detail (e.g., the witches' sabbath, a midnight assembly in fealty to the Devil). Moreover, this oft-reprinted volume was responsible for the misogynist association of witchcraft with women that became the dominant characteristic in the early modern period.

"Black" magic and its alleged practitioners often were persecuted, yet forms of "white" magic persisted in Europe on the boundaries between magic, mysticism, and emerging empiricism. During the Renaissance there was renewed interest in ancient Middle Eastern practices, Neoplatonic mysticism, and Arabic texts on alchemy and astrology. Pico della Mirandola sought hidden knowledge in Jewish Kabbala, a mystical practice for unlocking the divine secrets contained in written and unwritten Hebrew Scriptures. Marsilio Ficino studied astral magic and the power of music to channel cosmic influences, while Giordano Bruno explored the mystical traditions of Hermeticism, based on works of the legendary Alexandrian prophet of the 1st–3rd century Hermes Trismegistus. Although generally tolerated because their practices were perceived to be within the main Judaic

(continued on page 74)

(continued from page 73)

and Christian Hermetic tradition, practitioners of alchemy were sometimes considered to be evil magicians who acquired their knowledge through a pact with the Devil (as in the Faust legends).

Sebastian, and Prospero's brother, Antonio. With the arrival of the outsiders, the process of testing and eventual reconciliation begins. The party is brought to shore by Ariel, but Ferdinand is separated from the others and is believed drowned. Ariel helps foil plots against Prospero by Caliban and against Alonso by Antonio. Ariel then appears to Alonso and Antonio as a harpy and reproaches them for their treatment of Prospero. Alonso, believing Ferdinand dead, is certain that his death was punishment for Alonso's crime and has a change of heart. Prospero, convinced that Antonio and company are repentant (or at least chastened), reconciles all and prepares to return to Milan to reclaim his throne.

Young Ferdinand meantime has encountered Miranda, and the two have fallen instantly in love. Their courtship is watched carefully by Prospero, who, though insistent that they proceed carefully and preserve their virginity until they are actually married, welcomes this love relationship as a way of making Miranda happy and at the same time of reconciling Milan and Naples; their marriage will unite the two contending kingdoms.

The Tempest sums up much of what Shakespeare's mature art was all about. Once again the playwright presents a wifeless father with a daughter, in this case on a deserted island. Prospero behaves like a dramatist in charge of the whole play as well, masterminding his daughter's life and that of the other characters. The happy ending of the play will also mean an end to Prospero's career as artist and dramatist, for he is nearing retirement and senses that his gift will not stay with him forever.

The Tempest seems to have been intended as Shakespeare's farewell to the theatre. It contains moving passages of reflection on what his powers as artist have been able to accomplish, and valedictory themes of closure. As a comedy, it demonstrates perfectly the way that Shakespeare was able to combine precise artistic construction (the play chooses on this farewell occasion to observe the Classical unities of time, place, and action) with his special flair for stories that transcend the merely human and physical: *The Tempest* is peopled with spirits, monsters, and drolleries. This, it seems, is Shakespeare's summation of his art as comic dramatist.

Chapter 5

Shakespeare's English Contemporaries in Comedy

The first generation of professional playwrights in England has become known collectively as the university wits. Their nickname identifies their social pretensions, but their drama was primarily middle class, patriotic, and romantic. Their preferred subjects were historical or pseudo-historical, mixed with clowning, music, and love interest. At times, plot virtually evaporated; George Peele's *Old Wives' Tale* (*c.* 1595) and Thomas Nashe's *Summer's Last Will and Testament* (1600) are simply popular shows, charming medleys of comic turns, spectacle, and song. Peele was a civic poet, and his serious plays are bold and pageantlike; *The Arraignment of Paris* (1584) is a pastoral entertainment, designed to compliment Elizabeth. Robert Greene's speciality was comical histories, interweaving a serious plot set among kings with comic action involving clowns. In his *Friar Bacon and Friar Bungay* (1594) and *James IV* (1598), the antics of vulgar characters complement but also criticize the follies of their betters. Only John Lyly, writing for the choristers, endeavoured to achieve a courtly refinement. His *Gallathea* (1584) and *Endimion* (1591) are fantastic comedies in which courtiers, nymphs, and goddesses make rarefied love in intricate, artificial patterns, the very stuff of courtly dreaming.

In addition to Lyly, there were a number of playwrights that were in some respect influential in comedy and on Shakespeare's work. These include the somewhat older George Gascoigne, Ben Jonson, John Marston, and the coauthors Francis Beaumont and John Fletcher.

GEORGE GASCOIGNE

(b. *c.* 1539, Cardington, Bedfordshire, Eng.—d. Oct. 7, 1577, Barnack, near Stamford, Lincolnshire)

Gascoigne attended the University of Cambridge, studied law at Gray's Inn in 1555, and thereafter pursued careers as a politician, country gentleman, courtier, soldier of fortune, and man of letters, all with moderate distinction. He was a member of Parliament (1557–59). Because of his extravagance and debts, he gained a reputation for disorderly living. He served with English troops in the Low Countries, ending his military career as a repatriated prisoner of war. In 1575 he helped to arrange the celebrated entertainments provided for Queen Elizabeth I at Kenilworth and Woodstock and in 1576 went to Holland as an agent in the royal service. Among his friends were many leading poets, notably George Whetstone, George Turberville, and Edmund Spenser. Gascoigne himself was a worthy poet, and he pioneered in the use of several literary genres new to the English language.

He was a leader in drama as well. His *Jocasta* (performed in 1566) constituted the first Greek tragedy to be presented on the English stage. Translated into blank verse, with the collaboration of Francis Kinwelmersh, from Lodovico Dolce's *Giocasta*, the work derives ultimately from Euripides's *Phoenissae*. In comedy, Gascoigne's *Supposes* (1566?), a prose translation and adaptation of Ludovico Ariosto's *I Suppositi*, was the first prose comedy to be translated from Italian into English. A dramatically effective work, it provided the subplot for Shakespeare's

The Taming of the Shrew. *The Glasse of Government* (1575), is a didactic drama on the Prodigal Son theme.

JOHN LYLY

(b. 1554?, Kent, Eng.—d. November 1606, London)

Lyly was educated at Magdalen College, Oxford, and went to London about 1576. There he gained fame with the publication of two prose romances, *Euphues: The Anatomy of Wit* (1578) and *Euphues and His England* (1580), which together made him the most fashionable English writer of the 1580s. *Euphues* is a romantic intrigue told in letters interspersed with general discussions on such topics as religion, love, and epistolary style. Lyly's preoccupation with the exact arrangement and selection of words, his frequent use of similes drawn from classical mythology, and his artificial and excessively elegant prose inspired a short-lived Elizabethan literary style called "euphuism." The *Euphues* novels introduced a new concern with form into English prose, and Lyly is considered to be the first prose stylist to leave an enduring impression on the English language.

After 1580 Lyly devoted himself almost entirely to writing comedies. In 1583 he gained control of the first Blackfriars Theatre, in which his earliest plays, *Campaspe* and *Sapho and Phao*, were produced. All of Lyly's comedies except *The Woman in the Moon* were presented by the Children of Paul's, a children's company that was periodically favoured by Queen Elizabeth. The performance dates of his plays are as follows: *Campaspe* and *Sapho and Phao*, 1583–84; *Gallathea*, 1585–88; *Endimion*, 1588; *Midas*, 1589; *Love's Metamorphosis*, 1590; *Mother Bombie*, 1590; and *The Woman in the Moon*, 1595. All but one of these are in prose. The finest is considered to be *Endimion*, which some critics hold a masterpiece.

MASTER OF THE REVELS

From Tudor times up until the Licensing Act of 1737, an English court official called the Master of the Revels supervised the production and financing of often elaborate court entertainments. He later was the official issuer of licenses to theatres and theatrical companies and the censor of publicly performed plays.

A Master of the Revels was first appointed about 1495, and the Revels office soon developed a complicated system for building and painting spectacular scenery. In 1545 Sir Thomas Cawarden became master for life, and thereafter the office assumed importance. Decrees in 1581 and 1603 gave the Master of Revels licensing, censorship, and fee-collecting powers. The prestige of the office reached its high point during the mastership of Sir Henry Herbert (1623–42), after which England's theatres were closed during the Puritan interregnum. After the Restoration (1660), Herbert was reinstalled as master until his death in 1673, but the office was gradually stripped of its power. The Licensing Act of 1737 abolished it entirely, granting the power of censorship directly to the Lord Chamberlain. Although the Revels office did not have exclusive control over all court entertainment, the accounts and detailed records of the office are a valuable source for information on elaborate court productions from the 15th through the early 18th century.

Lyly's comedies mark an enormous advance upon those of his predecessors in English drama. Their plots are drawn from Classical mythology and legend, and their characters engage in euphuistic speeches redolent of Renaissance pedantry. But the charm and wit of the dialogues and the light and skillful construction of the plots set standards that younger and more gifted dramatists could not ignore.

Lyly's popularity waned with the rise of Thomas Kyd, Christopher Marlowe, and Shakespeare, and his appeals to Queen Elizabeth for financial relief went unheeded. He had hoped to succeed Edmund Tilney in the court post of Master of the Revels, but Tilney outlived him, and Lyly died a poor and bitter man.

BEN JONSON

(b. June 11?, 1572, London, England—d. Aug. 6, 1637, London)

The dramatist, lyric poet, and literary critic Ben Jonson is generally regarded as the second most important English dramatist, after William Shakespeare, during the reign of James I. Among his major plays are the comedies *Every Man in His Humour* (1598), *Volpone* (1605), *Epicoene; or, The Silent Woman* (1609), *The Alchemist* (1610), and *Bartholomew Fair* (1614).

THEATRICAL CAREER

Jonson was born two months after his father died. His stepfather was a bricklayer, but by good fortune the boy was able to attend Westminster School. His formal education, however, ended early, and he at first followed his stepfather's trade, then fought with some success with the English forces in the Netherlands. On returning to England, he became an actor and playwright, experiencing the life of a strolling player. He apparently played the leading role of Hieronimo in Thomas Kyd's *The Spanish Tragedy*. By 1597 he was writing plays for Philip Henslowe, the leading impresario for the public theatre. With one exception (*The Case Is Altered*), these early plays are known,

Portrait of the Jacobean dramatist Ben Jonson. As a literary critic, Jonson often found fault with the content of and language in Shakespeare's works. Universal Images Group/Getty Images

if at all, only by their titles. Jonson apparently wrote tragedies as well as comedies in these years, but only two of these are extant.

The year 1598 marked an abrupt change in Jonson's status, when *Every Man in His Humour* was successfully presented by the Lord Chamberlain's theatrical company (a legend has it that Shakespeare himself recommended it to them), and his reputation was established. In this play

COMEDY OF HUMOURS

The term derives from the Latin word *humor* (more properly *umor*), meaning "liquid," and its use in the medieval and Renaissance medical theory that the human body held a balance of four liquids, or humours: blood, phlegm, yellow bile (choler), and black bile (melancholy). When properly balanced, these humours were thought to give the individual a healthy mind in a healthy body.

In his play *Every Man Out of His Humour* (1599), Jonson explains that the system of humours governing the body may by metaphor be applied to the general disposition, so that a peculiar quality may so possess a person as to make him or her act in one way. Jonson's characters usually represent one humour and, thus unbalanced, are basically caricatures. Jonson distinguished two kinds of humour: one was true humour, in which one peculiar quality actually possessed a person, body and soul; the other was an adopted humour, or mannerism, in which a person attempted to appear singular by affecting certain fashions of clothing, speech, and social habits.

Jonson tried to bring the spirit and manner of Latin comedy to the English popular stage by presenting the story of a young man with an eye for a girl, who has difficulty with a phlegmatic father, is dependent on a clever servant, and is ultimately successful—in fact, the standard plot of the Latin dramatist Plautus. But at the same time Jonson sought to embody in four of the main characters the four "humours" of medieval and Renaissance medicine—choler, melancholy, phlegm, and blood—which were thought to determine human physical and mental makeup.

That same year Jonson killed a fellow actor in a duel, and, though he escaped capital punishment by pleading "benefit of clergy" (the ability to read from the Latin Bible), he could not escape branding. During his brief imprisonment over the affair he became a Roman Catholic.

Following the success of *Every Man in His Humour*, the same theatrical company acted Jonson's *Every Man Out of His Humour* (1599), which was even more ambitious. It was the longest play ever written for the Elizabethan public theatre, and it strove to provide an equivalent of the Greek comedy of Aristophanes; "induction," or "prelude," and regular between-act comment explicated the author's views on what the drama should be.

The play, however, proved a disaster, and Jonson had to look elsewhere for a theatre to present his work. The obvious place was the "private" theatres, in which only young boys acted. The high price of admission they charged meant a select audience, and they were willing to try strong satire and formal experiment. For them Jonson wrote *Cynthia's Revels* (*c.* 1600) and *Poetaster* (1601). Even in these, however, there is the paradox of contempt for human behaviour hand in hand with a longing for human order.

From 1605 to 1634 he regularly contributed masques for the courts of James I and Charles I, collaborating with the architect and designer Inigo Jones. This marked his favour with the court and led to his post as poet laureate.

JONSON'S MASQUES AT COURT

It appears that Jonson won royal attention by his *Entertainment at Althorpe*, given before James I's queen as she journeyed down from Scotland in 1603, and in 1605 *The Masque of Blackness* was presented at court. The "masque" was a quasi-dramatic entertainment, primarily providing a pretense for a group of strangers to dance and sing before an audience of guests and attendants in a royal court or nobleman's house. This elementary pattern was much elaborated during the reign of James I, when Jones provided increasingly magnificent costumes and scenic effects for masques at court. The few spoken words that the masque had demanded in Elizabethan days expanded into a "text" of a few hundred lines and a number of set songs. Thus the author became important as well as the designer: he was to provide not only the necessary words but also a special "allegorical" meaning underlying the whole entertainment. It was Jonson, in collaboration with Jones, who gave the Jacobean masque its characteristic shape and style. He did this primarily by introducing the suggestion of a "dramatic" action. It was thus the poet who provided the informing idea and dictated the fashion of the whole night's assembly.

PRIME AND LATER LIFE

In 1606 Jonson and his wife (whom he had married in 1594) were brought before the consistory court in London to explain their lack of participation in the Anglican church. He denied that his wife was guilty but admitted that his own religious opinions held him aloof from attendance. The matter was patched up through his agreement to confer with learned men, who might persuade him if they could. Apparently it took six years for him to decide to conform. For some time before this he and his wife had lived apart, Jonson taking refuge in turn with his patrons Sir Robert Townshend and Esmé Stuart, Lord Aubigny.

During this period, nevertheless, he made a mark second only to Shakespeare's in the public theatre. His comedies *Volpone; or, the Foxe* (1606) and *The Alchemist* (1610) were among the most popular and esteemed plays of the time. Each exhibited human folly in the pursuit of gold. Set respectively in Italy and London, they demonstrate Jonson's enthusiasm both for the typical Renaissance setting and for his own town on Europe's fringe. Both plays are eloquent and compact, sharp-tongued and controlled. The comedies *Epicoene* (1609) and *Bartholomew Fair* (1614) were also successful.

Jonson embarked on a walking tour in 1618–19, which took him to Scotland. During the visit the city of Edinburgh made him an honorary burgess and guild brother. On his return to England he received an honorary Master of Arts degree from Oxford University, a most signal honour in his time. Jonson's life was a life of talk as well as of writing. He engaged in "wit-combats" with Shakespeare and reigned supreme. It was a young man's ultimate honour to be regarded as a "son of Ben."

In 1623 his personal library was destroyed by fire. By this time his services were seldom called on for the entertainment of Charles I's court, and his last plays failed to please. In 1628 he suffered what was apparently a stroke and, as a result, was confined to his room and chair, ultimately to his bed. That same year he was made city chronologer (thus theoretically responsible for the city's pageants), though in 1634 his salary for the post was made into a pension. Jonson died in 1637 and was buried in Westminster Abbey.

The first folio edition of his works had appeared in 1616; posthumously, in a second Jonson folio (1640), appeared *Timber: or, Discoveries*, a series of observations on life and letters. Here Jonson held forth on the nature of poetry and drama and paid his final tribute to Shakespeare: in spite of acknowledging a belief that his great contemporary was, on occasion, "full of wind"—sufflaminandus erat—he declared that "I loved the man, and do honour his memory, on this side idolatry, as much as any."

JONSON ON SHAKESPEARE

During his own lifetime and shortly afterward, Shakespeare enjoyed fame and considerable critical attention. The English writer Francis Meres, in 1598, declared him to be England's greatest writer in comedy and tragedy. Writer and poet John Weever lauded "honey-tongued Shakespeare." Jonson, a literary critic in his own right, granted that Shakespeare had no rival in the writing of comedy, even in the ancient Classical world, and that he equaled the ancients in tragedy as well. But Jonson also faulted Shakespeare for having a mediocre command of the Classical languages and for ignoring Classical rules. Jonson objected when Shakespeare dramatized history extending over many years and moved his dramatic scene around from country to country, rather than focusing on 24 hours or so in a single location. Shakespeare wrote too glibly, in Jonson's view, mixing kings and clowns, lofty verse with vulgarity, mortals with fairies.

HIS PLAYS AND ACHIEVEMENT

Ben Jonson occupies by common consent the second place among English dramatists of the reigns of Elizabeth I and James I. He was a man of contraries. For "twelve years a papist," he was also—in fact though not in title—Protestant England's first poet laureate. His major comedies express a strong distaste for the world in which he lived and a delight in exposing its follies and vices. A gifted lyric poet, he wrote two of his most successful plays entirely in prose, an unusual mode of composition in his time. Though often an angry and stubborn man, no one had more disciples than he. He was easily the most learned dramatist of his time, and he was also a master of theatrical plot, language, and characterization. It is a measure of his reputation that his dramatic works were the first to be published in folio (the term, in effect, means the "collected works") and that his plays held their place on the stage until the period of the Restoration. Later they fell into neglect, though *The Alchemist* was revived during the 18th century, and in the mid-20th century several came back into favour: *Volpone, The Alchemist,* and *Bartholomew Fair* especially have been staged with striking success.

The Restoration dramatists' use of type names for their characters (Cockwood, Witwoud, Petulant, Pinchwife, and so on) was a harking back to Jonson, and similarly in the 18th century, with such characters as Peachum, Lumpkin, Candour, and Languish. And though, as the 18th century proceeded, comic dramatists increasingly used names quite arbitrarily, the idea of the Jonsonian "type" or "humour" was always at the root of their imagining. Jonson thus exerted a great influence on the playwrights who immediately followed him. In the late Jacobean and Caroline years, it was he, Shakespeare, and Francis Beaumont and John Fletcher who provided all the models. But it was he, and he alone, who gave the essential impulse to dramatic characterization in comedy of the Restoration and also in the 18th and 19th centuries.

JOHN MARSTON

(baptized Oct. 7, 1576, Oxfordshire, Eng.—d. June 25, 1634, London)

John Marston was educated at the University of Oxford and resided from 1595 at the Middle Temple, London. He began his literary career in 1598 with *The Metamorphosis of Pigmalions Image and Certaine Satyres*, an erotic poem in the newly fashionable Ovidian style. In the same year, the rough-hewn, obscure verses of *The Scourge of Villanie*, in which Marston referred to himself as a "barking satirist," were widely acclaimed.

In 1599 Marston began writing for the theatre, producing *Histrio-mastix* (published in 1610), probably for performance at the Middle Temple. In his character Chrisoganus, a "Master Pedant" and "translating scholler," the audience was able to recognize the learned Ben Jonson. A brief, bitter literary feud developed between Marston, Jonson, and Thomas Dekker, all of whom wrote for rival children's companies (organized groups of boy actors)—part of what is known as "the war of the theatres." In *Poetaster* (produced 1601) Jonson depicted Marston as Crispinus, a character with red hair and small legs who was given a pill that forced him to disgorge a pretentious vocabulary.

For the Children of Paul's theatre company, Marston wrote *Antonio and Mellida* (1600); its sequel, *Antonio's Revenge* (1601); and *What You Will* (1601). The most memorable is *Antonio's Revenge*, a savage melodrama of a political power struggle with elements of parody and fantasy.

In 1604 Marston transferred his allegiance to the boy company at the Blackfriars Theatre (i.e., the Children of the Queen's Revels, later Children of the Blackfriars), for which he wrote his remaining plays. *The Dutch Courtezan* (produced 1603–04) as well as *The Malcontent* (1604) earned him his place as a dramatist. The former, with its coarse, farcical counterplot, was considered one of the cleverest comedies of its time. Although Marston used all the apparatus of contemporary revenge tragedy in *The Malcontent*, the wronged hero does not kill any of his tormentors and regains power by sophisticated Machiavellian stratagems.

In 1605 Marston collaborated with Jonson and with George Chapman on *Eastward Ho*, a comedy of the contrasts within the life of the city. But the play's satiric references to opportunistic Scottish countrymen of the newly crowned James I gave offense, and all three authors were imprisoned.

After another imprisonment in 1608, presumably once again for libel, Marston left unfinished *The Insatiate Countesse*, his most erotic play, and entered the Church of England. He took orders in 1609, married the daughter of James I's chaplain, and in 1616 accepted an ecclesiastical post in Christchurch, Hampshire. In 1633 he apparently insisted upon the removal of his name from the collected edition of six of his plays, *The Workes of John Marston*, which was reissued anonymously the same year as *Tragedies and Comedies*.

BEAUMONT AND FLETCHER

The best-known Jacobean playwright-collaborators were Francis Beaumont and John Fletcher. Their collaboration lasted for some seven years (1606–13). Although scholars now believe that they wrote 10 or fewer plays together, they wrote well together, and their association was particularly fruitful.

The masterpieces of the Beaumont and Fletcher collaboration—*Philaster*, *The Maides Tragedy*, and *A King and No King*—show, most clearly in the last, the emergence of most of the features that distinguish the Fletcherian mode from that of Shakespeare, George Chapman, or John Webster: the remote, often pseudohistorical, fairy-tale setting; the clear, smooth speech rising to great emotional arias of declamatory rhetoric; the basically sensational or bizarre plot that faces the characters with wild "either–or" choices between extremes and that can be manipulated toward a sad or a happy ending as the playwrights choose; and the sacrifice of consistency and plausibility in characterization so that patterns can be made out of constantly shifting emotional states and piquant situations can be prolonged.

FRANCIS BEAUMONT

(b. *c.* 1585, Grace-Dieu, Leicestershire, England—d. March 6, 1616, London)

The son of Francis Beaumont—justice of common pleas of Grace-Dieu priory, Charnwood Forest, Leicestershire—Beaumont entered Broadgates Hall (later Pembroke College), Oxford, in 1597. His father dying the following year, he abruptly left the university without a degree and later (November 1600) entered London's

Francis Beaumont, engraving. © Photos.com/Thinkstock

Inner Temple, where he evidently became more involved in London's lively literary culture than in legal studies.

In 1602 there appeared the poem *Salmacis and Hermaphroditus,* generally attributed to Beaumont, a voluptuous and voluminous expansion of the Ovidian legend that added to the story humour and a fantastic array of episodes and conceits. At age 23 he prefixed to Ben Jonson's *Volpone* (1607) some verses in honour of his "dear friend" the author. John Fletcher contributed verses to the same volume, and, by about this time, the two were collaborating on plays for the Children of the Queen's Revels. According to the antiquarian John Aubrey, in *Brief Lives*,

> They lived together on the Banke side, not far from the Play-house, both batchelors; lay together...; had one wench in the house between them...; the same cloathes and cloake, &c., betweene them.

In 1613 Beaumont married an heiress, Ursula Isley of Sundridge in Kent, and retired from the theatre. He died in London in 1616 and was buried in Westminster Abbey.

Scholars now know that *The Knight of the Burning Pestle* is Beaumont's unaided work. For the rest, attempts to separate the shares of Beaumont and Fletcher in any given work are complicated by the fact that Beaumont sometimes revised scenes by Fletcher and Fletcher edited some of Beaumont's work. *The Knight of the Burning Pestle* parodies a then popular kind of play—sprawling, episodic, with sentimental lovers and chivalric adventures. It opens with The Citizen and his Wife taking their places on the stage to watch "The London Merchant"—itself a satire on the work of a contemporary playwright, Thomas Dekker. Citizen and Wife interrupt, advise, and insist that the play should be more romantic and their apprentice should take a leading part. Thereafter these two contradictory plots go forward side by side, allowing Beaumont to have fun with bourgeois naïveté about art.

JOHN FLETCHER

(baptized Dec. 20, 1579, Rye, Sussex, England—d. Aug. 29, 1625, London)

John Fletcher's father, Richard Fletcher, was minister of the parish in which John was born and became afterward queen's chaplain, dean of Peterborough, and bishop successively of Bristol, Worcester, and London, gaining a measure of fame as an accuser in the trial of Mary, Queen of Scots, and as the chaplain sternly officiating at her execution. When not quite 12, John was apparently admitted pensioner of Corpus Christi College, Cambridge, and two years later became a Bible clerk. From the time of his father's death (1596) until 1607, when he, like Beaumont, contributed a poem to Jonson's *Volpone*, little is known of his life.

Fletcher began to work with Beaumont at first for the Children of the Queen's Revels and its successor and then (from *c.* 1609 until Beaumont's retirement in 1613) mainly for the King's Men at the Globe and Blackfriars theatres. After 1613, when Beaumont married and retired from the theatre, Fletcher often collaborated with or had his plays revised by Philip Massinger, who actually succeeded him in 1625 as chief playwright of the King's Men. Nathan Field, William Rowley, and even Shakespeare himself (in *The Two Noble Kinsmen*) were other collaborators. Throughout his career Fletcher also wrote plays unaided. He died in the London plague of 1625 that killed some 40,000 others. The aforementioned Aubrey claimed that Fletcher had lingered in the city to be measured for a suit of clothes instead of making his escape to the country.

John Fletcher, one-half of the duo of Beaumont and Fletcher. Universal Images Group/Getty Images

Of Fletcher's unaided plays, the best are perhaps *The Loyall Subject* and *A Wife for a Moneth,* the latter a florid and loquacious play, in which a bizarre sexual situation is handled with cunning piquancy, and the personages illustrate clearly Fletcher's tendency to make his men and women personifications of vices and virtues rather than individuals. The best of Fletcher's comedies, for urbanity and consistency of tone, is probably *The Wild-Goose Chase*, an episodic play that is alive with irony and easy wit.

Lastly, there are the Fletcherian plays in which others besides Beaumont had a hand. *Wit at Several Weapons* is a comedy that might have been written wholly by Thomas Middleton. *The Captaine* (to which Beaumont may have contributed) is a lively, complex play of sexual intrigue, with tragic dilemmas, too. Notable among the numerous plays in this group are *The False One* and *The Beggars Bush* The former is an original, incisive, and moderately subtle treatment of the story of Caesar and Cleopatra, which may well have aided John Dryden to compose *All for Love* and for which the greater credit goes to Massinger. The latter is worth reading for its "version of pastoral," which genially persuades the audience that it is better to be a country beggar than a tyrannical king.

Chapter 6

Shakespeare's Playhouse

The theatre to which Shakespeare's name is attached is London's Globe Theatre. After 1599, all of his plays—and some plays by others as well—were produced there.

Early in 1599 Shakespeare, who had been acting with the Lord Chamberlain's Men since 1594, paid into the coffers of the company a sum of money amounting to 12.5 percent of the cost of building the Globe. He did so as a chief shareholder in the company, and by doing so he helped to establish a uniquely successful form of commercial operation for the actors of the time. This investment gave Shakespeare and the other leading actors both a share in the company's profits and a share in their playhouse.

At this time, officially approved playhouses and officially approved acting companies had been in existence in London for only five years. The Lord Chamberlain's Men was one of only two companies licensed to perform within the London city limits. The other company used the Rose playhouse, owned by an impresario and his ex-actor son-in-law.

THE SECOND BEST PLAYHOUSE

Shakespeare's company built the Globe only because it could not use the special roofed facility, Blackfriars Theatre, that James Burbage (the father of their leading actor, Richard Burbage) had built in 1596 for it inside the city. The elder Burbage had a long history as a theatrical entrepreneur. In 1576 he had built the first successful amphitheatre, known as The Theatre, in a London suburb. Twenty years later, when the lease on The Theatre's land was about to expire, he built the theatre in Blackfriars as its replacement. But the wealthy residents of Blackfriars persuaded the government to block its use for plays, so Burbage's capital was locked up. He died early in 1597, his plans for the future of theatre in London frustrated.

Thus, the members of the Lord Chamberlain's Men were forced to rent a playhouse. At the end of 1598, they decided to build one for themselves. Because the inheritance of Burbage's sons, Cuthbert and Richard, was tied up in the Blackfriars, they formed a consortium with Shakespeare and four other actors, who became co-owners of the new Globe. The same shortage of cash made the

Actor Sir Ian McKellen pointing to an excavation site believed to contain the foundations of The Theatre, the first successful amphitheatre in London. The site was unearthed in 2008. Tim Whitby/Getty Images

consortium reluctant traditionalists; they gave up the idea of an indoor theatre in the city. The old playhouse was one of their few remaining resources, but they could not use it in situ because the lease had expired, so they dismantled it, took the timbers (illegally) to make the skeleton of their new amphitheatre, and kept the basic auditorium shape of The Theatre for the new building.

THE SUCCESS OF THE GLOBE

For all its hurried construction in 1599, the Globe proved a triumph. Its first decade of use made it a favourite not just with subsequent generations of theatregoers but with the company itself. In later years the troupe paid a lot to keep it going. At least two circumstances provide evidence for this statement. In 1608, when the company could finally fulfill James Burbage's original plan for the Blackfriars, the members chose, extravagantly, to operate the two theatres together, using the open-air Globe in the summer and the roofed Blackfriars in the winter. Had they chosen to, they easily could have rented one of the buildings to another company, since there was a shortage of playhouses in London in this period. But they kept both for themselves. They were given a second chance to transfer full-time to the Blackfriars in 1613, when the Globe burned to the ground, its thatch accidentally set alight by a cannon during a performance of *Henry VIII*. By then the Blackfriars was already beginning to bring better profits than the Globe, since the smaller house size was more than compensated by its higher prices. Instead, bearing the cost out of sentiment and traditional loyalty, the company members dug deep into their own pockets and rebuilt the Globe more splendidly than before.

Technically, the 1599 Globe and its 1614 replacement span an era in the history of theatre design. The first Globe, based on the skeleton of the original Theatre of 1576, was unique not just as the most famous example of that peculiar and short-lived form of theatre design but because it was actually the first to be built specifically for an existing acting company and financed by the company itself. Shakespeare designed *As You Like It*, *Hamlet*, *Twelfth Night*, *Othello*, *All's Well That Ends Well*, *Measure for Measure*, *King Lear*, *Macbeth*, *Antony and Cleopatra*, *Coriolanus*, *Pericles*, and *The Winter's Tale*, not to mention *Troilus and Cressida* and *Timon of Athens*, for performance there.

THE DESIGN OF THE GLOBE

The design of the original Theatre responded to a mix of traditions. Its name, which up to then had been used for atlases (such as Mercator's) rather than for playhouses, drew attention to the Roman theatre tradition. Its circular shape, though, reflected not the D-shape of a Roman amphitheatre but the gatherings of crowds in a circle around the actors in town marketplaces, where all the players of 1576 got their training. The concept of building a scaffold with three levels of galleries surrounding a circular yard mimicked the arrangement for audiences of existing bearbaiting and bullbaiting houses. The stage, a platform mounted in the yard, was the kind of thing that traveling companies set up in inn yards.

The old Theatre was a 20-sided structure, as near to a circle as Elizabethan carpentry could make it. It stood more than 30 feet (9 metres) high, with three levels of seating in its galleries. Audience access was either through two narrow passageways under the galleries into the standing room of the yard around the stage or up two external stair towers into the rear of the galleries. Five of the 20 bays of the galleries were cut off by the frons scenae, or tiring-house wall, behind which the actors kept

View across the stage of the rebuilt Globe Theatre, showing one of two posts securing the stage cover and the amphitheatre's three-tiered gallery. The Bridgeman Art Library/Getty Images

their store of props, costumes, and playbooks and prepared themselves for their performances. The stage was a 5-foot- (1.5-metre-) high platform protruding from the tiring-house into the middle of the yard. Two posts upheld a cover over the stage that protected the players and their expensive costumes from rain. The audience standing in the yard had no cover, though when it rained they could pay more and take shelter in the lowest gallery.

The Globe reproduced this old shape, with a few innovations mainly in the fresh painting and decoration of the stage area. Each of the four London amphitheatres that scholars know most about, the Rose, the Swan, the Globe, and the Fortune, had auditorium bays of a certain size, about 10 feet 6 inches (roughly 3 metres) from front to back and an average width of 14 feet (about 4 metres). The Globe and Fortune, and probably the Swan, had 20 bays in all, while the smaller Rose had 14. Seating in the form of degrees (wooden benches raked upward to the rear), along with the roofing over the topmost gallery, provided all the comfort short of a cushion that Elizabethans expected. A few rooms were reserved for the most privileged on the stage balcony itself. Including the space for nearly a thousand customers to stand in the yard around the stage, the small Rose had a total capacity of about 2,400 people, while contemporary estimates of total audience capacity at the Swan and the Globe claimed 3,000.

The stage was large, 43 or 44 feet (about 13 metres) across and 27 or more feet (some 8 metres) deep. The two stage posts were substantial, since they had to uphold the large cover, or heavens, which had a trapdoor in it with a windlass for winding boys playing gods down onto the stage. Below the heavens trapdoor was one in the stage, which served as the entry point for King Hamlet's ghost and the grave for Ophelia. The tiring-house wall had two doors on its flanks for entrances and exits and a central

RICHARD TARLTON

(b. Condover, Shropshire, Eng.—d. Sept. 3, 1588, London)

Richard Tarlton takes his place in theatrical history as creator of the stage yokel. His performance in this role is thought to have influenced Shakespeare's creation of the character Bottom in *A Midsummer Night's Dream*, and Tarlton himself is said to have been the model for the court jester Yorick described in *Hamlet*. Tarlton's popularity and genius were undisputed. Thomas Nashe wrote that audiences began "exceedingly to laugh when he first peept out his head"; Edmund Spenser mourned him as "our pleasant Willy...with whom all joy and jolly merriment/ Is also deaded"; and in 1643 Sir Richard Baker said that "for the... Clown's part he never had his match, never will have." Few of his actual roles as a comedian are known, however. Contemporary sketches show Tarlton in country homespun, holding a pipe and tabor and standing on one toe.

Tarlton is first mentioned in 1570 for his didactic ballad on the "late great floods." The Stationers' Register of 1576 credits him with "a newe booke in Englishe verse intituled Tarltons Toyes." By 1579 he was a well-known actor and Queen Elizabeth I's favourite jester, the only one able to "undumpish" her when she was out of humour and the only one allowed to tell her of her faults. In 1583 he became a leading comic actor of the Queen's Men and groom of Her Majesty's chamber. His plays, which were praised by contemporaries, are all lost. Of later jestbooks that were published as Tarlton's, such as *Tarltons Newes out of Purgatorie* (*c.* 1590) and *Tarlton's Jests* (1611), most are of dubious authenticity, but, like inn signboards that depicted him as late as 1798, they attest to the endurance of his fame.

opening, normally covered by a set of hangings (Polonius's arras) that concealed the caskets in *The Merchant of Venice* and Hermione's statue in *The Winter's Tale*. Above the three openings, a balcony ran the width of the stage wall, the central room of which was used for scenes that required an upper window or balcony or the walls of a town.

PLAYING AT THE GLOBE

The experience of watching a performance at the Globe was radically different from that of viewing modern Shakespeare on-screen. The plays were staged in the afternoons, using the light of day, and the audience surrounded the stage on all sides. No scenery was used, except for occasional emblematic devices such as a throne or a bed. It was almost impossible not to see the other half of the audience standing behind the players. Consequently, much of the staging was metatheatrical, conceding the illusory nature of the game of playing and making little pretense of stage realism.

REBUILDING THE GLOBE

The Globe was pulled down in 1644, two years after the Puritans closed all theatres, to make way for tenement dwellings. In 1970 the American actor Sam Wanamaker, who was driven by the notion of reconstructing a replica of the Globe, established the Shakespeare Globe Playhouse Trust. Seventeen years later a groundbreaking ceremony was held on a Bankside site near that of the original Globe, and in 1989 the foundations of the original building were discovered buried beneath a historic 19th-century building. Although only a small percentage of the original theatre could be examined, the discovery

WILLIAM KEMPE

(b. *c.* 1560–d. *c.* 1603)

William Kempe (Kemp) was one of the most famous clowns of the Elizabethan era. Much of his reputation as a clown grew from his work as a member of the Chamberlain's Men (*c.* 1594–99), of which he was an original member. Kempe was also renowned as a dancer of jigs.

The first record of Kempe as a performer is with the Earl of Leicester's Men on a tour of the Low Countries and Denmark in 1585–86. As a solo performer, he followed in the tradition of Richard Tarlton and took on many of Tarlton's famous roles after the great clown's death in 1588. Kempe performed with Lord Strange's Men in *A Knack to Know a Knave*, which he may

Woodcut showing Elizabethan clown William Kempe (right) *doing what he did best, dancing.* Time & Life Pictures/Getty Images

(continued on page 104)

(continued from page 103)

have helped to write, in 1592. By this time Kempe's reputation as a dancer was well established. He had enormous energy and stamina, and his improvised jigs (usually performed after a play) ranged from the wildly ridiculous to the overtly sexual.

With the Chamberlain's Men, Kempe originated several of Shakespeare's best known characters, including Dogberry in *Much Ado About Nothing* and Peter in *Romeo and Juliet*. He was also believed to have played Bottom in *A Midsummer Night's Dream*, Lancelot Gobbo in *The Merchant of Venice*, and Falstaff. Kempe's name, however, disappears from the lists of the company in 1599. The reason for his departure is not clear, though it has been speculated that his penchant for improvising (when Hamlet warns the players to "let those that play your clowns speak no more than is set down for them," the reference may be to Kempe) and his earthy jigs may not have appealed to the more refined audience the company was trying to cultivate.

After leaving the Chamberlain's Men, Kempe remained in the public eye, gaining notoriety for performing a morris dance from London to Norwich (about 100 miles north) in February 1600. He again toured the continent in 1601 and then joined Worcester's Men upon his return. It is thought that he died of the plague in London soon after.

of these foundations enabled scholars to make certain design adjustments. They changed the planned 24 sides to 20, for instance, and, using the angles revealed by the archaeologists, they made the whole polygon 99 feet (30 metres) in outside diameter. By referring to a number of extant Elizabethan buildings for clues to the structure, style, interior, and roofing, scholars and architects completed the design of the Globe Theatre reconstruction. Using traditional methods and materials, with only a few

Replica of the late 16th-century Globe Theatre, completed in 1997, London. © david hughes/Fotolia

concessions to modern fire regulations and the like, builders completed work on the new theatre in the mid-1990s. It is now part of a larger complex of buildings known as the International Shakespeare Globe Centre.

The new theatre is not a perfect replica of the original building. It is made, for example, from new green oak, like the Fortune, not from the 23-year-old timbers of a dismantled building, like the original Globe. Its design is still speculative in key areas, such as its size, the shape of the stage, and the decorations. In addition, certain compromises had to be made to satisfy the constraints of contemporary fire-safety regulations. These entailed making the stairways and access doors wider, increasing

Nighttime view of the reconstructed Globe Theatre (completed in 1997) from across the River Thames, London. © microimages/Fotolia

the number of entrances to the yard, positioning sprinkler valves in the ridging of the thatched gallery roofing, and including conduits for electrical wiring. These provisos—and a restriction on the size of the audience at any performance to a maximum of 1,600, roughly half the number that attended the original Globe—have secured the right for the new Globe to be used once again as a theatre.

The basic justification for attempting to reconstruct the Globe in a faithful version of the original is that it can be used to learn more about Shakespeare's plays. The Globe was Shakespeare's machine, financed and built by the company that intended to use it. How it worked and

ROBERT ARMIN

(b. *c.* 1568—d. November 1615, London, Eng.)

Actor and playwright Robert Armin was an apprentice to a goldsmith in the 1580s. It was during this time that he befriended Richard Tarlton, one of the most famous clowns of the time. Tarlton recognized Armin's comic genius and made him his protégé. Armin's early acting experience included a stint with Lord Chandos's Men as well as solo performances. His books about these experiences were *Foole upon Foole; or, Six Sortes of Sottes*, about six household fools, and *Quips upon Questions,* a collection from his masterly performances where he extemporized verse responses to audience questions; both were published in 1600 under the pseudonym Clonnico de Curtanio Snuffe. Armin wrote the play *The History of the Two Maids of More-clacke* (1609), and a book of ballads entitled *The Italian Taylor and His Boy* (1609).

Armin succeeded the famous William Kempe as the primary clown performer with the Chamberlain's Men. Among his earliest roles with the company were Dogberry in *Much Ado About Nothing* and Touchstone in *As You Like It.* The latter role may have been written expressly for Armin. His unique verbal skills allowed him to transcend the country rustics that had been the specialty of Tarlton and Kempe. With Armin in mind, Shakespeare created fools that were sharp-tongued and often wiser than the more noble characters. In addition to Touchstone, Armin originated many witty fools, including Feste in *Twelfth Night* and the Fool in *King Lear*. It is believed that he also performed as Abel Drugger in Ben Jonson's *The Alchemist* and as Robin in Christopher Marlowe's *Doctor Faustus.* Armin was listed as one of the principal players in the First Folio.

what it produced have a great deal to offer to students of Shakespeare's plays—those written pre-texts, as they have been called with some justice, which record all he thought his fellows needed to know when they staged his plays. Everything that has been wrung from these pre-texts in the last four centuries is enhanced by a better knowledge of Shakespeare's original concept.

Conclusion

Shakespeare's early comedies share the popular and romantic forms used by other playwrights of the age—the university wits—but overlay them with elements of elegant, courtly fun and a keen understanding of comedy's fragility and artifice. These are festive comedies, giving access to a society vigorously and imaginatively at play. The plays of one group—*The Comedy of Errors*, *The Taming of the Shrew*, *The Merry Wives of Windsor*, and *Twelfth Night*—are comedies of intrigue, fast-moving, often farcical, and placing a high premium on wit. The plays of a second group—*The Two Gentlemen of Verona*, *Love's Labour's Lost*, *A Midsummer Night's Dream*, and *As You Like It*—have as a common denominator a journey to a natural environment, such as a wood or a park, in which the restraints governing everyday life are released and the characters are free to remake themselves untrammeled by society's forms, their surroundings providing a space in which the fragmented individual may recover wholeness.

All the comedies share a belief in the positive, health-giving powers of play, but not one is completely innocent of doubts about the limits that encroach upon the comic space. In the four plays that approach tragicomedy—*The Merchant of Venice*, *Much Ado About Nothing*, *All's Well That Ends Well*, and *Measure for Measure*—festivity is in direct collision with the constraints of normality, with time, business, law, human indifference, treachery, and selfishness. These plays give greater weight to the less-optimistic perspectives on society current in the 1590s, and their comic resolutions are openly acknowledged to be only provisional, brought about by manipulation, compromise, or the exclusion of one or more major characters.

The last group of plays comprises the four romances—*Pericles*, *Cymbeline*, *The Winter's Tale*, and *The Tempest*—which deal with the whims of fortune and trials by suffering. In these plays Shakespeare's imagination returns to the popular romances of his youth and dwells on mythical themes—wanderings, shipwrecks, the reunion of families torn apart, and the resurrection of people long thought dead. There is consolation here, of a sort, beautiful and poetic, but still the romances do not turn aside from the actuality of suffering, chance, loss, and unkindness. Shakespeare's subsidiary theme in these plays is a sustained examination of the nature of his own art—and how only the omniscient, controlling author can make these comfortable resolutions possible. Even in this unearthly context a subtle interchange is maintained between the artist's delight in his illusion and his mature awareness of his own disillusionment.

Glossary

amphitheatre An oval or circular building with rising tiers of seats ranged about an open space.

buffoon A gross and often uneducated person who acts in a ridiculous manner.

burlesque A literary or dramatic work that seeks to ridicule by means of extreme exaggeration or comic imitation.

chide To scold or voice disapproval.

churl A rude, surtly person.

counterpoint The use of contrast or interplay of elements in an artistic work, including drama.

denouement The final outcome of the main dramatic complication in a literary work.

farce A light dramatic composition marked by broadly satirical comedy and improbable plot.

gallery An outdoor balcony of a theatre, such as the Globe, in which patrons were seated.

grotesque Bizarre or unnatural.

incongruous Not in agreement with generally accepted principles; incompatible.

prosaic Dull or ordinary.

realism In drama, showing action on stage that is as true to nature or to real life as possible, without idealization.

renunciation To actively and, often, vocally deny oneself something.

repartee A series of witty remarks between two or more people, or characters in a show.

rustic Lacking in social graces or refinement; considered more suited for the country than the city.

satire A literary or dramatic work holding up human vices and follies to ridicule or scorn.

sentimental comedy A form of comedy that addresses itself to the spectator's love of goodness rather than to his sense of humour, and emphasizes the moral aspects of its situations.

suitor Someone who tries to attract a woman, with the hope of marrying her.

sundry Various and many.

windlass A machine used for hoisting or hauling something or, in the case of theatre, someone.

Bibliography

Late 20th- and early 21st-century collections of Shakespeare's works include Irving Ribner and George Lyman Kittredge (eds.), *The Complete Works of Shakespeare* (1971); Sylvan Barnet (ed.), *The Complete Signet Classic Shakespeare* (1972); Stanley Wells and Gary Taylor (eds.), *William Shakespeare, The Complete Works*, 2nd ed. (2005); G. Blakemore Evans and J.J. Tobin (eds.), *The Riverside Shakespeare*, 2nd ed. (1997); David Bevington (ed.), *The Complete Works of Shakespeare*, 6th ed. (2009); and Stephen Greenblatt (ed.), *The Norton Shakespeare* (2008). Three series were in progress at the turn of the 21st century, with plays and poems in individual volumes: Stanley Wells (ed.), *The Oxford Shakespeare* (1982–); Philip Brockbank (ed.), *The New Cambridge Shakespeare* (1984–); and Richard Proudfoot, Ann Thompson, and David Scott Kastan (eds.), *The Arden Shakespeare*, 3rd series (1995–).

Studies of Shakespeare and comedy are all but innumerable. They include Robert G. Hunter, *Shakespeare and the Comedy of Forgiveness* (1965); Arthur Kirsch, *Shakespeare and the Experience of Love* (1981); Alexander Leggatt, *Shakespeare's Comedy of Love* (1974, reprinted 1990); W. Thomas MacCary, *Friends and Lovers: The Phenomenology of Desire in Shakespearean Comedy* (1985); and Leo Salingar, *Shakespeare and the Traditions of Comedy* (1974).

Studies that consider Shakespeare's comedies broadly include Robert S. Miola, *Shakespeare and Classical Comedy: The Influence of Plautus and Terence* (1994). Penny Gay, *The Cambridge Introduction to Shakespeare's Comedies* (2008); Michael Mangan, *A Preface to Shakespeare's Comedies, 1594–1603* (1996); Gary F. Walter, *Shakespeare's Comedies*

(1991); Ronald P. Draper, *Shakespeare, the Comedies* (2000); Ejner J. Jensen, *Shakespeare and the Ends of Comedy* (1991); Frances N. Teague (ed.), *Acting Funny: Comic Theory and Practice in Shakespeare's Plays* (1994); Clarice Swisher (ed.), *Readings on the Comedies* (1997); and Ronald R. Macdonald, *William Shakespeare: The Comedies* (1992).

Other studies of aspects of Shakespeare and comedy are Camille Wells Slights, *Shakespeare's Comic Commonwealths* (1993); Penny Gay, *As She Likes It: Shakespeare's Unruly Women* (1994); Martin D. Yaffe, *Shylock and the Jewish Question* (1997); Anthony J. Lewis, *The Love Story in Shakespearean Comedy* (1992); Michael D. Friedman, *The World Must Be Peopled: Shakespeare's Comedies of Forgiveness* (2002); Michael J. Collins, *Shakespeare's Sweet Thunder: Essays on the Early Comedies* (1997); Stuart M. Tave, *Lovers, Clowns, and Fairies: An Essay on Comedies* (1993); Emma Smith (ed.), *Shakespeare's Comedies* (2004); and Northrup Frye, *The Myth of Deliverance: Reflections on Shakespeare's Problem Comedies* (1993).

Index

G

H

J

K

L

M

P

Q

R

S

T

W